QUICK
crocheted
accessories

3
skeins
or less

Sharon Zientara

INTERWEAVE.
interweave.com

EDITOR Michelle Bredeson

TECHNICAL EDITOR Charles Voth

ART DIRECTOR Charlene Tiedemann

COVER DESIGN Charlene Tiedemann

INTERIOR DESIGN & LAYOUT
JoAnn Dickey

PHOTOGRAPHER Joe Hancock

PHOTO STYLIST Katie Himmelberg

HAIR AND MAKEUP Kathy MacKay

PRODUCTION Katherine Jackson

Interweave
A division of F+W, A Content
and eCommerce Company
4868 Innovation Drive
Fort Collins, CO 80525
interweave.com

Manufactured in China
by RR Donnelley Shenzhen.

Library of Congress
Cataloging-in-Publication Data

Zientara, Sharon, author.

3 skeins or less : quick crocheted
accessories / Sharon Zientara.

    pages cm

Includes index.

ISBN 978-1-62033-798-1 (pbk.)
ISBN 978-1-62033-799-8 (PDF)

1. Crocheting--Patterns. I. Title.
II. Title: Three skeins or less.

TT825.Z527 2015

746.43'4--dc23

2014036870

10 9 8 7 6 5 4 3 2 1

Acknowledgments

Thank you *to everyone at Interweave for entrusting me with such a great concept. To Allison Korleski, Michelle Bredeson, and Karin Strom: your continued partnership is truly a joy. Thank you for all of the generous support from the many amazing yarn companies whose fibers made such beautiful canvases. Thank you to all the designers whose projects grace these pages, with special recognition due to Terri Keller for your generosity and lightning-fast sample crocheting. Thank you to the entire Makers' Mercantile family for enduring my frenzied creative process. Finally, thank you to my amazing motley crew of friends and family, for without you I would be a lonely spinster with too many cats and mountains of yarn.*

Contents

Yarnville
BUTTON FARM
STITCH ROW
CROCHET WAY
Loopy Lane
COTTON HOLLOW

Introduction

Everything in life moves along so quickly these days. I think that this is one of the chief reasons why the movement toward handmade items has seen so much success in recent years. The idea of creating something that takes time, care, and thoughtful consideration is a virtue in a time of dashed-off text messages, emails, and one-click Internet transactions. But this doesn't mean that you have to spend a huge amount of time, money, or effort to satisfy this impulse to create something by hand. The feeling that you put into choosing the perfect fiber or yarn color and the love that goes into each stitch are the same no matter how big the project or how long it takes to make. The (near) instant gratification comes built in to these pages. Each pattern in this collection is a relatively quick piece that takes three skeins or less of yarn to create, and many of the projects can be crocheted in an evening or two. The love and care is something only you can supply. I hope you find yourself reaching for this book time and again with that thought in mind.

HAPPY MAKING, STITCHING, SHARING, AND GIVING.

Sharon

Buttons & Lace Hat

DESIGNED BY SHARON ZIENTARA

This project was designed to showcase two of my favorite things: hats and buttons. I could spend hours in front of a button wall picking the perfect combination. I chose the stitch pattern on the brim because the lacy openings create built-in buttonholes—no extra steps are required. Just sew on buttons and wear this hat anywhere!

FINISHED SIZE
19" in circumference × 9" tall (48.5 × 23 cm).

YARN
Sportweight (#2 Fine)

Shown here: Blue Sky Alpacas Sport Weight (100% alpaca; 110 yd [101 m]/1¾ oz [50 g]): #504 light tan, 2 skeins.

HOOK
Size F/5 (3.75 mm)

NOTIONS
Yarn needle; stitch markers; darning thread; four ¾" (2 cm) buttons.

GAUGE
30 sts and 10 rows = 4" (10 cm) in shell st pattern. 25 sts and 24 rows = 4" (10 cm) in sc.

NOTES
Brim of hat is crocheted flat and stitches are picked up around brim to form crown. Crown is worked in spirals. Place marker (pm) in beg st of rnd to keep track of rnds.

2 SKEINS

Hat Band

Ch 32.

Row 1: Sc in 2nd ch from hook, *sk next 2 ch, 7 dc in next ch, sk next 2 ch, sc in next ch; rep from * across, turn.

Row 2: Ch 4 (counts as tr), sk (sc, first dc) *dc in each of next 5 dc**, sk next 3 sts; rep from * across, ending last rep at **, sk next dc, tr in last sc, turn.

Row 3: Ch 3 (counts as dc), 3 dc in tr at base of ch, sc in center dc of next 5-dc group, *sk next 2 dc, 7 dc bet last skipped st and next st, sk next 2 dc, sc in next dc; rep from * across to last 3 sts, sk next 2 dc, 4 dc in top of turning ch, turn.

Row 4: Ch 3 (counts as dc), sk first dc, dc in each of next 2 dc, *sk next 3 sts, dc in each of next 5 dc; rep from * across to last 6 sts, sk next 3 sts, dc in each of next 2 dc, dc in top of turning ch, turn.

Row 5: Ch 1 (does not count as st), sc in first dc, *sk next 2 dc, 7 dc bet last skipped st and next st, sk next 2 dc, sc in next dc; rep from * across ending with sc in top of turning ch, turn.

Rep Rows 2–5 until piece measures 19" (48.5 cm), ending with a Row 5.

Body

Work 115 sts evenly around as follows:

Rnd 1: Ch 1 (does not count as st), sc in same st as join, pm in beg st, (ch 1, sc in row end) evenly around—58 sc, 57 ch-sps.

Rnd 2: Ch 1, sk first sc, (sc in next ch-1 sp, ch 1, sk next sc) around, sc in first ch-1 sp to join. Move marker to first sc.

Rnd 3: (Ch 1, sk next sc, sc in next ch-sp) around, moving marker up each rnd to first sc made.

Rep Rnd 3 until crown measures 2" (5 cm) from band, or until desired length.

Crown

Rnd 1: *(Ch 1, sk next sc, sc in next ch-1 sp) 10 times, ch 1, pm in ch just made, sk next (sc, ch 1, sc), sc in next ch-1 sp, rep from * around—52 sc, 51 ch-sps.

Rnd 2: Sc in first ch-1 sp, (ch 1, sk next sc, sc in next ch-1 sp) around, moving markers to ch worked after sc has been worked in marked ch-sps.

Dec rnd: Ch 1, sk next sc, (sc in next ch-1 sp, ch 1, sk next sc) around to and in marked ch-sp, sk next (ch 1, sc), sc in next ch-1 sp; rep from * around, moving markers to ch worked over sk sts.

Rep last 2 rnds 4 more times, then rep dec rnd 7 times.

Fasten off leaving a long tail to sew top of hat closed. Block to measurements.

Finishing

With coordinating darning thread and yarn needle, sew buttons to placket of hat band, matching up buttons to shell openings in hat band st pattern. Edge of hat should overlap by one row of shell pattern.

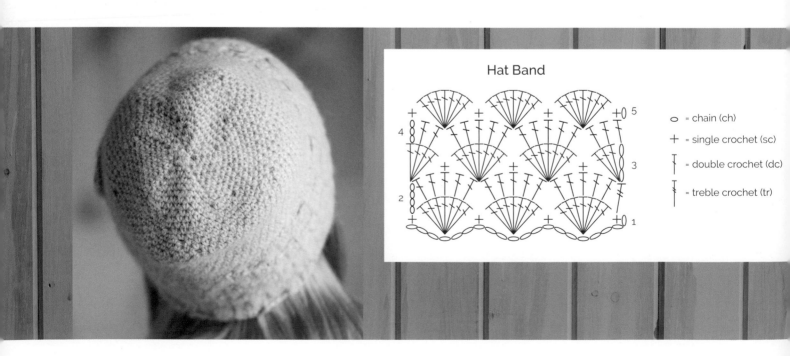

Hat Band

o = chain (ch)

+ = single crochet (sc)

= double crochet (dc)

= treble crochet (tr)

Corona Cowl

DESIGNED BY BRENDA K. B. ANDERSON

This cowl was inspired by the stackable jelly bracelets of the 1980s. It's fun to watch each tube stripe up in a new color. The cowl is also easy to customize by simply removing or adding tubes.

FINISHED SIZE
Size S with directions for sizes M and L in parentheses. Each tube measures about 22" (56 cm) in circumference and about ¾" (2 cm) tall. Sample is shown with 8 tubes. Cowl will stretch at least 2" (5 cm) in circumference to fit over the head. Button strap measures 8 (9, 10)" (20.5 [23, 25.5] cm) long, including about 2" (5 cm) of overlap when buttoned.

YARN
Sportweight (#2 Fine)

Shown here: Zitron Unisono (100% virgin superwash wool; 328 yd [300 m]/3½ oz [100 g]): #1203, 2 skeins. Yarn distributed by Skacel Collection, Inc.

HOOK
Size F/5 (3.75 mm). Adjust hook size if necessary to obtain correct gauge.

NOTIONS
Stitch marker (m); yarn needle; 1½" (3.8 cm) button; embroidery needle or sewing needle and thread (if the button holes are too small for an embroidery needle and yarn to fit through).

GAUGE
20 sts and 14 rounds = 4" [10 cm] in hdcbb stitch pattern worked in the round. You can also check your gauge by working 1 tube and checking the fit. (See Note.)

NOTE
Each tube is made beginning with a long foundation chain. The first row is worked into the bottom of the chain, and the remainder of the tube is worked in the round without joining. A round of sl sts will attach the foundation row to the last row worked, creating a hollow tube.

2 SKEINS

Half double crochet through the back bar (hdcbb): This is just a regular hdc st made into the back bar of the previous round of sts. The back bar is the horizontal strand on the WS of a hdc st situated about halfway between the top and bottom of the stitch. When you work into this stitch, the RS will be facing you and you will tilt the work towards you to see the back of the hdc, you will slide your hook through the bar from top to bottom (in a downward motion), yo, and pull up a loop, yo, and draw through all 3 loops on hook.

Tube (make 8)

Ch 121.

Row 1: Beg with second ch from hook and working in bottom bump of ch, hdc in each of next 120 sts—120 sts. Place st marker (pm) in top of beg hdc. Do not join.

Rnd 2: Beg with the marked st, and being careful not to twist the strip of crochet, 1 hdcbb (see Stitch Guide) in each st around—120 sts.

Rnds 3–7: Hdcbb in each st—120 sts.

Rnd 8: 2 hdcbb sts in beg st (to reposition the working lp), ch 1, turn work so WS is facing, fold work with WS tog (foundation ch is directly in front of last rnd worked), sl st these two edges tog by working under the front lp of foundation ch (the edge in front) and at the same time, under the back bar of the last rnd worked (the edge in back). When working into back bar, insert hook under back bar in an upward motion—from bottom to top. Make sure that sl sts are loose as to not affect the elasticity of the tube. Fasten off leaving a 10" (25.5 cm) yarn tail. Use yarn needle and yarn tails to sew the little holes closed at beg of rnds. Weave in ends. Lightly block only if necessary.

Button Strap

Strap is designed to fit 4–6 (7–9, 10–12) tubes and measures 8 (9, 10)" (20.5 [23, 25.5] cm) in length, including a 2" (5 cm) overlap.

Ch 39 (45, 51).

Row 1: Leave long beg tail (to sew button on), starting with 12th ch from hook, and working in bottom bump, sc in each of the next 28 (34, 40) chs.

Rnd 2: Keeping the same side facing, rotate piece 180 degrees to work in opposite side of foundation ch, 2 hdc in each of next 2 sts (pm in first hdc of rnd to keep track of beg of rnds), hdc in each of the next 26 (32, 38) sts, 18 hdc in ch-lp, hdc in each of the next 26 (32, 38) sts, 2 hdc in each of the next

2 sts—78 (90, 102) sts. Do not join, but continue to work in the rnd with RS facing.

Rnd 3: [2 hdcbb in each of the next 2 sts, hdcbb in each of the next 35 (41, 47) sts, 1 hdcbb into each of the next 2 sts] twice—86 (98, 120) sts.

Rnd 4: [2 hdcbb in each of the next 2 sts, hdcbb in each of the next 39 (45, 51) sts, 1 hdcbb in each of the next 2 sts] twice—94 (106, 118) sts.

Rnd 5: [2 hdcbb in each of the next 2 sts, hdcbb in each of the next 43 (49, 55) sts, 1 hdcbb in each of the next 2 sts] twice—102 (114, 126) sts.

Rnd 6: Sl st in the back bar of each st around. Make sure that sl sts are loose enough so they will not constrict the edges of the button strap.

Fasten off.

Finishing

Block lightly if necessary.

Use embroidery needle and beg yarn tail to sew button to RS of button strap. The center of the button should match up with the point where this yarn tail comes out of the fabric. Weave in ends.

Wrap button strap around tubes and fasten button.

Honeycomb Shawlette

DESIGNED BY REGINA RIOUX

This geometric shawl can be made as a series of motifs, which are then joined, or using the join-as-you-go method. Either way, the construction and size is entirely up to you! The border motifs could be eliminated for a very pretty, graphic-looking scarf, or you could sew underarm seams and wear this like a shrug over a summer dress.

FINISHED SIZE
About 13" tall × 32" wide
(33 × 81.5 cm), buttoned.

YARN
DK weight (#3 Light)

Shown here: Berroco Weekend DK (75% acrylic, 25% cotton; 268 yd [247 m]/3½ oz [100 g]): #2964 curry, 3 hanks.

NOTIONS
Yarn needle; 4 toggles.

HOOK
Size G/6 (4 mm).

GAUGE
1 motif measures 2½" (6.5 cm) from point to point.

3 SKEINS

Motif (make 108)

Ch 24, sl st to first ch to join rnd.

Rnd 1: Ch 2, 2 sc, (sc, ch 2, sc) in next st, [sc in next 3 sts, (sc, ch 2, sc) in next st] 5 times, sc, sl st in beg ch 2 to join rnd.

Rnd 2: Ch 1, sc in next 4 sts, (sc, ch 2, sc) in ch-2 sp, [sc in next 5 sts, (sc, ch 2, sc) in ch-2 sp] 5 times, sc, sl st to first sc to join rnd. Fasten off.

Joining Motifs (Join-as-You-Go Method)

Use the diagram as a guide for motif placement. Motifs are joined together on Rnd 2 at the corner (ch 2) spaces.

Join a working motif with a completed motif at corners as follows: Replace a traditional motif corner (sc, ch 2, sc) with (sc, ch 2, remove hook from working st and insert hook from front to back through desired corner of finished motif, insert hook back into working st and pull up a lp through the corner of finished motif, ch 2, sc in working corner of working motif). After completion of first motif, all remaining motifs will have a combination of traditional corners and join-as-you-go corners.

Shawlette Edging

Attach yarn with a sl st at bottom front of shawlette and work the following edge pattern:

Ch 1, [sc in next st, ch 3, sl st in first ch, (picot made), sk next st] across entire edge of shawlette adding button detailing to front of shawlette per instructions (below).

When edging rnd is complete, sl st to first sc made on rnd. Fasten off.

Finishing

Weave in ends. Block. Sew on toggles.

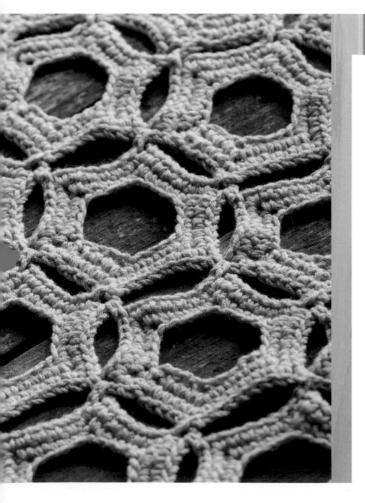

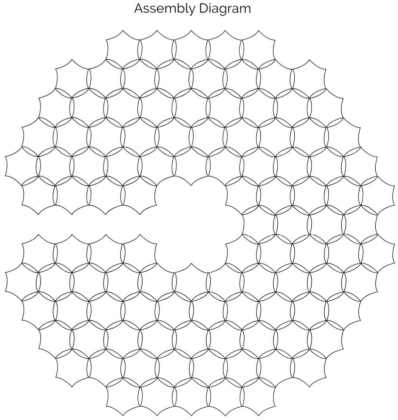

Assembly Diagram

Mosaic Slippers

DESIGNED BY CRISTINA MERSHON

These slippers work up quickly for a great last-minute gift. Each motif takes only a few minutes to make, and sewing them together will help hone your finishing skills. The self-striping yarn changes color as you stitch each motif, creating a fun surprise.

FINISHED SIZE
The pattern adapts easily from a size adult 5 through 9 by varying the hook size. For size adult 5, use a size D/3 (3.25 mm) hook to create a 3" × 3" (7.5 × 7.5 cm) square motif. For size adult 7, use a size E/4 (3.5 mm) hook to create a 3¼" × 3¼" (8.5 × 8.5 cm) square motif. For size adult 9, use a size F/5 (3.75 mm) hook to create a 3½" × 3½" (9 × 9 cm) square motif. Sample shown is size adult 9.

YARN
Worsted weight (#4 Medium)

Shown here: Wisdom Yarns Poems (100% wool; 109 yd [100 m]/1¾ oz [50 g]): #587 peacock, 2 skeins. Yarn distributed by Universal Yarn.

HOOK
See Finished Size, above. Adjust hook size if necessary to obtain correct size motif.

GAUGE
See Finished Size, above.

NOTE
Each slipper is constructed using 6 square motifs joined together (see assembly diagram). So you will need 12 square motifs to make a pair.

2 SKEINS

Motif (make 12)

Make an adjustable ring (see Glossary).

Rnd 1: Ch 3, 19 dc in ring, sl st to top of beg ch-3 to join. Pull yarn tail to tighten the adjustable ring until no opening is visible—20 dc.

Rnd 2: Ch 1, sc blo in next 2 dc, *(sc blo, ch 2, sc blo) in next dc**, sc blo in next 4 dc; rep from * around ending final rep at **, sc blo in next dc, sl st in beg ch—24 sc, 4 ch-sps.

Rnd 3: Ch 3, dc blo in next 3 sc, *(2 dc, ch 3, 2 dc) in ch-sp**, dc blo in next 6 sc; rep from * around ending final rep at **, dc in next 3 sc, sl st in beg ch. Fasten off. Weave in ends.

Edging

Sew the motifs together following the assembly diagram and using mattress stitch (see Glossary). The sts are worked in the back of the dc sts so that both lps of the top of the st face the RS of the fabric.

Rnd 1: Join in any stitch of slipper opening with (sl st, ch 1, sc) in every st around, sl st in beg ch.

Rnd 2: Ch 2, hdc blo in every sc across until the end of the rnd, sl st in beg ch.

Rnd 3: Ch 1, reverse sc blo in every hdc across until the end of the rnd, sl st in beg ch. Fasten off. Weave in ends.

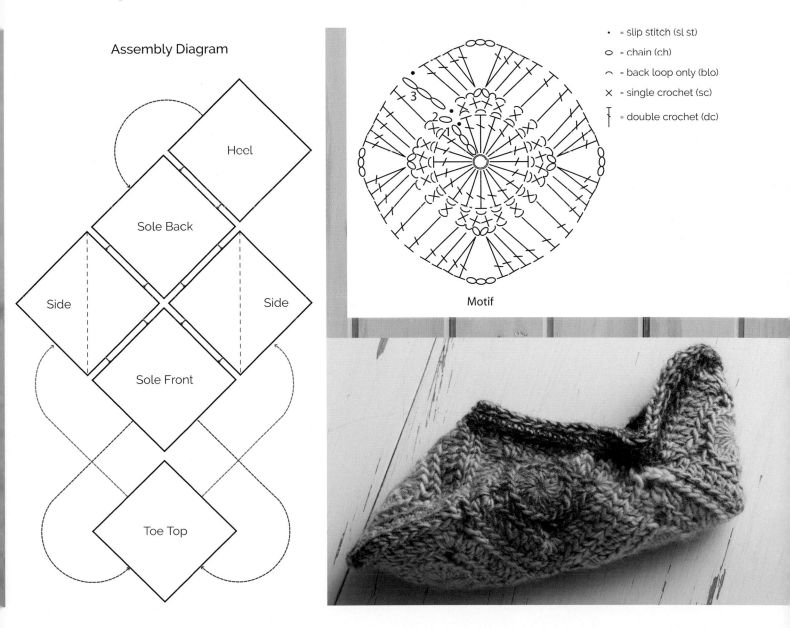

Assembly Diagram

Heel

Sole Back

Side   Side

Sole Front

Toe Top

Motif

- • = slip stitch (sl st)
- ○ = chain (ch)
- ⌒ = back loop only (blo)
- ✕ = single crochet (sc)
- † = double crochet (dc)

Long Winter's Scarf

DESIGNED BY BRENDA K. B. ANDERSON

This classic muffler is made in a stitch pattern that even the pickiest of guys (or gals!) will love. The slip stitches make a very warm, flexible, and smooth fabric that closely resembles knitting. A gradient yarn creates just enough (but not too much) visual interest and allows you to watch the colors change as you stitch.

FINISHED SIZE
68" × 5½" (173 × 14 cm) after block
ing (not including fringe).

YARN
Worsted weight (#4 Medium)

Shown here: Schoppel Wolle
Gradient (100% wool; 284 yd
[260 m]/3½ oz [100 g]): #1535
blues, 2 balls.

HOOK
Size L/11 (8 mm). Adjust hook size
if necessary to obtain correct
gauge.

NOTIONS
Stitch markers (m); yarn needle; a
piece of cardboard that measures
5" (12.5 cm) tall by about 6" or 7"
(15 or 18 cm) wide for making
fringe.

GAUGE
15 sts and 24 rows = 4" (10 cm) in
sl st worked in back lps only.

NOTE
Scarf is worked sideways in
turned rows.

2 SKEINS

Scarf

Ch 221. If you lose track of the number of stitches you have chained, just chain on a few extras—it is better to have too many than not enough. You can count your stitches again on the next row, placing a stitch marker every 20 sts or so in case you lose track. If you chained too many, just unravel the stitches that you do not need after you work the first row.

Row 1: Starting with the 2nd ch from hook and working in bottom ridge lp of ch, sl st in each of the next 220 sts. Place marker (pm) in first and last st of each row so that you do not miss stitches at the ends of rows.

Rows 2–32: Ch 1, turn, sl st blo into each st across—220 sts.

Fasten off.

Finishing

Weave in ends. Wet block, stretching the scarf a few inches lengthwise can help even out your work.

Fringe

CUT FRINGE

Wrap yarn around the narrower dimension of the cardboard piece 64 times for 4 pieces of yarn in each fringe group (or 48 times if you want to use 3 pieces of yarn in each fringe group).

Note: This is only enough fringe for one end of the scarf. Slide one blade of the scissors next to the edge of the cardboard and all of the yarn lps. Each piece of yarn should measure about 10" (25.5cm) in length. Set aside and repeat this process for the other end of the scarf.

ATTACH FRINGE

Attach a group of fringe to the end of every other row of scarf. In other words, each ridge of the scarf should get a group of fringe attached to the end of it. Insert hook through a ridge at the end of scarf and leave it there while you get the cut fringe in order. Fold 4 (or 3) strands of cut yarn in half to find the center. Place center of yarn group across throat of hook. Holding all of the ends of the fringe together with one hand, and the hook in the other hand, pull the center of all 4 (or 3) strands (held together) through the scarf. Make this lp big enough to reach through it with your fingers (or a hook) and pull all of the cut ends through. Carefully pull on yarn to tighten lp. Try to make the ends as even as possible. Repeat process for each ridge across each end of the scarf. Trim up to 1" (2.5 cm) off the bottom edge of fringe to even it out.

Arcadian Wrap

DESIGNED BY KATHY MERRICK

This gorgeous, rustic wrap, inspired by a region in Greece, is a statement piece in more ways than one. Each motif is different from the next, and, while we have laid out the construction, you could easily switch it up. Additionally, each ball of yarn is unique as it is first knit up on a machine, hand painted, and then unwound back into a ball, making for fascinating color changes.

FINISHED SIZE
67" long × 24" at the widest point (170 × 61 cm) after blocking.

YARN
Fingering weight (#1 Super Fine)

Shown here: Schoppel Wolle XL Kleckse Cat Print Hand Dyed (100% wool, 437 yd [400 m]/3½ oz [100 g]): #2190 ecru, 2 balls. Yarn distributed by Skacel Collection, Inc.

HOOK
Size E/4 (3.5 mm). Adjust hook size if necessary to obtain correct gauge.

GAUGE
Motif #1: 8" (20.5 cm) diameter, #2: 6" (15 cm) diameter, #3: 8" (20.5 cm) diameter, #4: 7" (18 cm) diameter, #5: 8" (20.5 cm) diameter, #6, 7" (18 cm) diameter, #7: 5" (12.5 cm) diameter, #8: 6" (15 cm) diameter, #9: 7" (18 cm) diameter.

NOTES
Wrap is made up of 3 each of 9 different motifs attached together. Join motifs on last round of each according to diagram.

2 SKEINS

Motif #1

Ch 12, sl st to first ch to form ring.

Rnd 1: Ch 1, 24 sc into ring, sl st to first sc.

Rnd 2: Ch 7 (counts as first dtr), *sk 1 sc, dtr, ch 5, dc into 2nd yo of dtr. Rep from * 10 times, ending with dc into 4th ch of ch-7 sp at beg of rnd, ch 2, dc in top of ch-7 sp.

Rnd 3: Ch 1, sc into side of last dc, *ch 7, sc in next ch-5 sp. Rep from * 11 times, sl st in first sc of rnd.

Rnd 4: Sl st in first ch-7 sp, ch 1; ([7 sc, ch 5] in next ch-sp) 11 times; 7 sc in last ch-7 sp; ch 2, dc in first sc of rnd.

Rnd 5: Ch 8 (counts as dc, ch-5), *sc into center sc of 7 sc of previous rnd; 5 dc into next ch-5 sp, ch 5. Rep from * 11 times, ending with 4 dc in ch-2 sp at beg of rnd, sl st to 3rd ch at beg of rnd.

Rnd 6: Ch 1, [(sc, ch 3, 4 dc) in ch-5 sp, ch 5] 12 times, ending with sl st in sc at beg of rnd.

Fasten off.

Motif #2

Ch 8, sl st to first ch to form ring.

Rnd 1: Ch 3 (counts as first dc), 17 dc in ring, sl st to top of ch-3 sp at beg of rnd.

Rnd 2: Ch 1, sc in top of ch-3 sp, *ch 12, turn. Sc in 2nd ch from hook, sc, 2 hdc, 7 dc; sk 2 dc of Rnd 1, sc; rep from * 5 times, ending with sl st in first sc at beg of rnd. Fasten off.

Motif 1

Motif 2

Rnd 3: Sl st in opposite side of 4th ch of first "petal" to join. Ch 4 (counts as first [dc, ch 1] of rnd); *[sk 1, dc in next st, ch 1] 3 times, dc in end of petal, ch 1, dc in first sc, ch 1, dc in next sc, [ch 1, sk 1, dc in next st] 3 times**, sk (3 dc, sc, 3 dc), dc into opposite side of 4th ch of next "petal"; rep from * around, ending with sl st in 3rd ch of ch-4 sp at beg of rnd.

Rnd 4: Ch 1, sc in first ch-1 sp of Rnd 3, *(ch 3, sc in ch-1 sp) 4 times; ch 5, sc in same sp; (ch 3, sc in ch-1 sp) 4 times; sc in next ch-1 sp; rep from * 5 times, ending with sl st in first sc of rnd. Fasten off.

Motif #3

Ch 6, sl st to first ch to form ring.

Rnd 1: Ch 1, 12 sc in ring, sl st to first sc.

Rnd 2: Ch 8 (counts as first dc, ch-5), *sk next sc, (dc, ch 5); rep from * 5 times, ending with sl st to 3rd ch at beg of rnd.

Rnd 3: Ch 1, (7 sc in next ch-sp) 6 times, ending with sl st to first sc of rnd.

Rnd 4: Sl st in first 2 sc from Rnd 3. Ch 3 (counts as first dc), 4 dc, ch 4; * sk 2 sc, 5 dc, ch 4; rep from * 4 times, ending with sl st in top of ch 3 sp at beg of rnd.

Rnd 5: Sl st to 2nd dc of Rnd 4. Ch 3 (counts as first dc), 2 dc; *ch 3, dc in ch-4 sp of Rnd 4, ch 3, sk 1 dc, 3 dc; rep from * 4 times, ending with sl st in top of ch-3 sp at beg of rnd.

Rnd 6: Ch 3 (counts as first dc), 2 dc, *ch 5, sc in first ch-3 sp of Rnd 5, ch 3, sc in next ch-3 sp of Rnd 5, ch 5, 3 dc; rep from * 5 times, ending with sl st in top of ch-3 sp at beg of rnd.

Rnd 7: Ch 3 (counts as first dc), sk dc, dc in next dc; *ch 6, sc in ch-5 sp in Rnd 6, ch 3, sc in ch-3 sp in Rnd 6, ch 3, sc in next ch-5 sp, ch 5, dc, sk dc, dc in next dc; rep from * 5 times, ending with sl st to top of ch 3 sp at beg of rnd.

Rnd 8: Ch 3, dc in next dc (counts as first dc2tog), *ch 9, sc in next ch 3 sp of

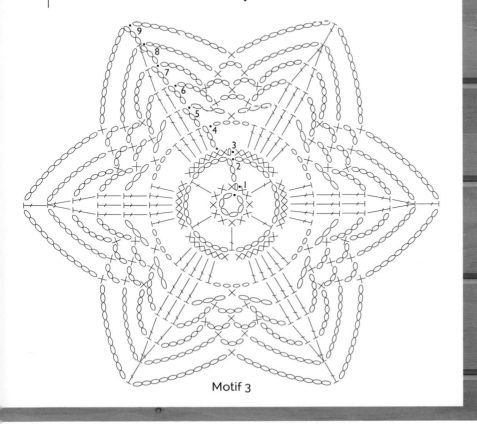

Motif 3

- • = slip stitch (sl st)
- ∽ = chain (ch)
- ✕ = single crochet (sc)
- ⊤ = half double crochet (hdc)
- ⊤ = double crochet (dc)
- ⊤ = treble crochet (tr)
- ⊤ = double treble crochet (dtr)
- ⊤ = double treble crochet (dtr)
- ⊤ = triple treble crochet (trtr)
- ⊤ = sextuple treble crochet (str)
- ⬗ = 3 double crochet cluster (3dc-cl)
- ⬗ = 4 treble crochet cluster (4tr-cl)

Rnd 7, ch3, sc in next ch-3 sp, ch 9, dc-2tog (see Glossary) rep from *, ending with sl st in first dc2tog at beg of rnd.

Rnd 9: Ch 14 (counts as dc, ch 11), *sc in next ch-3 sp of Rnd 8, ch 11, dc, ch 11; rep from * 5 times, ending with ch 11, sl st to 3rd ch at beg of rnd. Fasten off.

Motif #4

Ch 7, sl st to first ch to form ring.

Rnd 1: (Ch 3, dc2tog in ring) to make first dc3tog, (ch 8, dc3tog in ring [see Glossary]) 5 times, ch 8, end with sl st to first dc3tog of rnd.

Rnd 2: Ch 1, *sc in dc3tog of Rnd 1, ch 7, dc4tog (see Glossary) in ch-8 sp of Rnd 1, ch 7, sc in dc3tog of Rnd 1; rep from * 5 times, ending with sl st to first sc of rnd.

Rnd 3: Ch 1, *sc in sc of Rnd 2, ch 8, sc in dc4tog, ch 8; rep from * 4 times, ending with sc in last sc, ch 8, sc in dc4tog, str (see Stitch Guide) in first sc of rnd.

Rnd 4: Ch 1, *sc in sc of Rnd 3, ch 9, dtr in next sc, ch 9; rep from * 5 times, ending with sl st in first sc of rnd.

Rnd 5: Ch 1, *sc in sc of Rnd 4, (ch 7, dtr in next ch-9 sp) 2 times, ch 7, dtr in dtr of Rnd 4, (ch 7, dtr in next ch-9 sp) 2 times, ch 7; rep from * 5 times, ending with sl st in first sc of rnd. Fasten off.

Motif #5

Ch 5, sl st to first ch to form ring.

Rnd 1: Ch 6 (counts as first dc, ch 3), (dc in ring, ch 3) 5 times, sl st to 3rd ch at beg of rnd.

Rnd 2: Ch 6 (counts as dc, ch 3), dc in same st, *ch 6, (dc, ch 3, dc) in next dc; rep from * 5 times, ending with ch 2, dc in 3rd ch at beg of rnd.

Rnd 3: Ch 1, sc in dc of Rnd 2; *ch 3, 5 dc in next ch-3 sp, ch 3, sc in next ch-5 sp of Rnd 2, ch 3; rep from * 5 times, ending with sl st in first sc of rnd.

Rnd 4: Ch 1, *sc in next sc of Rnd 4, ch 6, (dc, ch 4, dc) in 3rd dc of next 5-dc group, ch 6; rep from * 5 times, ending with ch 3, dc in first sc of rnd.

Rnd 5: Ch 1, sc in dc of Rnd 4, *ch 5, sc in next ch-6 sp of Rnd 4, ch 3, 7 dc (cluster) in next ch-4 sp, ch 3, sc in next ch-6 sp; rep from * 5 times, ending with sl st in first sc of rnd.

Rnd 6: 2 sl st in ch-5 sp of Rnd 5, ch 1,

Motif 4

Motif 5

sc in same sp. *Ch 5, sc in first dc of next 7dc-group, ch 5, (sc, ch 5, sc) in 4th dc of 7dc-group, ch 5, sc in last dc of 7dc-group, ch 5, sc into next ch-5 sp of Rnd 5; rep from * 5 times, ending with sl st in first sc of rnd. Fasten off.

Motif #6

Ch 8, sl st to first ch to form circle.

Rnd 1: Ch 5 (counts as first dc, ch 2), (dc in ring, ch 2) 5 times, ending with sl st to 3rd ch at beginning of rnd.

Rnd 2: Ch 1, sc into same space. *3 dc into next ch-2 sp, sc into next sc; rep from * 5 times, ending with sl st to first sc of rnd.

Rnd 3: Ch 1, *sc into next sc, ch 5; rep from * 5 times, ending with ch 2, dc

into first sc of rnd.

Rnd 4: Ch 1, sc into dc of Rnd 3, *ch 3, dc3tog into next sc, ch 3, sc into next ch-5 sp of Rnd 3, ch 3; rep from * 5 times, ending with sl st into first sc of rnd.

Rnd 5: Ch 1, *sc into next sc, ch 3, (dc-3tog, ch3, dc3tog) into next dc3tog of Rnd 4, ch 3; rep from * 5 times, ending with sl st into first sc of rnd.

Rnd 6: Sl st in each of next 4 sts to first dc3tog of Rnd 5, (ch 3, dc2tog) into first dc3tog of Rnd 5 (counts as first dc-3tog), ch 3, dc3tog into next ch-3 sp of Rnd 5, ch 3, dc3tog into next dc3tog of Rnd 5, ch 3, * dc3tog into next dc3tog, ch 3, dc3tog into next ch-3 sp, ch 3, dc-3tog into next dc3tog, ch 3. Rep from * 4 times, ending with sl st to top of ch-3 sp at beg of rnd.

Rnd 7: Sl st into next ch-3 sp of Rnd 6, 4 sc into next ch-3 sp of Rnd 6, 3 sc into each remaining ch-3 sp of Rnd 6.

Rnd 8: Ch 1, *sc into next sc, ch 3, sk 2 sc, dc2tog into next 2 sc, picot, ch 3, sk 2 sc; rep from * 10 times. Fasten off.

Motif #7

Ch 6, sl st to first ch to form circle.

Rnd 1: Ch 1, (sc, ch 3, tr, ch 3) 6 times, ending with sl st to first sc of rnd.

Rnd 2: Sl st in each of next 4 sts to top of next tr of Rnd 1, (ch 12, dc into 4th ch, ch 3, sl st into next tr) 6 times, ending with dc into first sl st of rnd.

Rnd 3: Ch 3, ([dc, hdc, 7 sc, hdc, dc] into

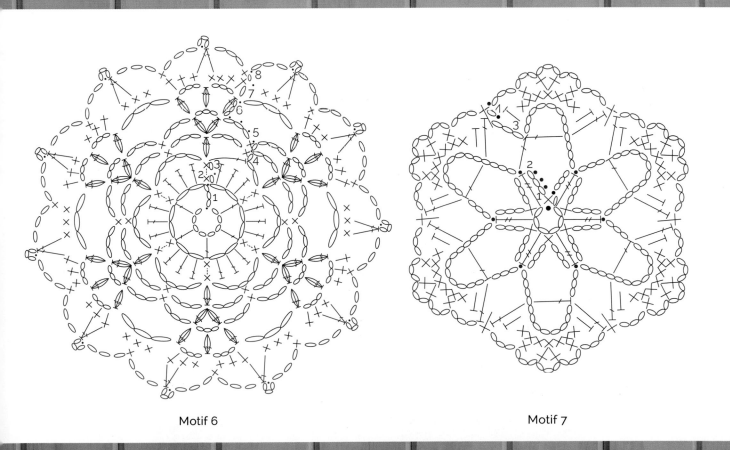

Motif 6

Motif 7

next ch-sp) 6 times, ending with sl st into ch-3 sp at beg of rnd.

Rnd 4: Ch 1, sc in between ch-3 sp and first dc of Rnd 3; *ch 3, sk 3, sc into next st, ch 3, sk 1 st, (sc, ch 3, sc) into next st, sk 1 st, ch 3, sc into next st, ch 3, sc in between next 2 dc; rep from * 5 times, ending with sl st to first sc of rnd. Fasten off.

Motif #8

Ch 10, sl st to first ch to form circle.

Rnd 1: Ch 3 (counts as first dc), 23 dc into circle. Sl st to top of ch-3 sp at beginning of rnd.

Rnd 2: Ch 1, sc into ch-3 sp of Rnd 1, (sc into next dc, ch 9, sc into next dc) 11 times, ch 4, dtr (see Glossary) into first sc of rnd.

Rnd 3: Ch 1, 3 sc into dtr of Rnd 2, *3 sc into top of next ch-9 lp, 6 sc into side of same lp,

6 sc into side of next lp, 3 sc across top of same lp; rep from * 5 times, ending

with 7 sc into final lp, sl st to first sc.

Rnd 4: Ch 1, (6 sc across top of next joined lps, ch 7) 6 times, ending with sl st to first sc of rnd.

Rnd 5: Ch 1, *sc into next sc, ch 4, sk 4 sc, sc into next sc, ch 8, sl st into sc before ch 4, turn, 13 sc into ch-8 lp, 11 sc into next ch-7 sp of Rnd 4; rep from * 5 times, ending with sl st in first sc of rnd. Fasten off.

Motif 8

Motif 9

- • = slip stitch (sl st)
- o = chain (ch)
- ✕ = single crochet (sc)
- ⊤ = half double crochet (hdc)
- ⊺ = double crochet (dc)
- ⊺ = treble crochet (tr)
- ⊧ = double treble crochet (dtr)
- ⊧ = triple treble crochet (trtr)
- ⊧ = sextuple treble crochet (str)
- = 3 double crochet cluster (3dc-cl)
- = 4 treble crochet cluster (4tr-cl)

Motif #9

Ch 6, sl st to first ch to form ring.

Rnd 1: Ch 5 (counts as first dc, ch 2), (dc, ch 2) 11 times into ring. Sl st to top of ch-3 sp at beg of rnd.

Rnd 2: Ch 3 (counts as first dc), (2 dc into next ch-2 sp, dc into next dc) 11 times, 2 dc into last ch-2 sp. Sl st to top of ch-3 sp at beg of rnd.

Rnd 3: Ch 1, sc into top of ch-3 of Rnd 2, (ch 3, sk 1 dc, sc into next dc) 17 times, ending with ch 1, hdc into first sc at beg of rnd.

Rnd 4: Ch 1, sc into hdc of Rnd 3, (ch 5, sc into next ch-3 sp) 17 times, ending with ch 2, dc in first sc at beg of rnd.

Rnd 5: Ch 1, sc into dc of Rnd 4, ([dc, ch 5, tr, ch 5, tr, ch 5, dc] into next ch-5 sp, sc into next ch-5 sp, ch 5, sc in next ch-5 sp) 6 times, ending with sl st to first sc at beg of rnd.

Rnd 6: Ch 1, (6 sc into next ch-5 sp, [sc, hdc, 4 dc, ch 5, 4 dc, hdc, sc] into next ch-5 sp, 6 sc into next ch-5 sp, 6 sc into next ch-5 sp) 6 times, ending with sl st to first sc at beg of rnd. Fasten off.

Wrap

Make Motif #1.

Make Motif #2, joining to Motif #1 on Rnd 4 with sl st from two points.

Make Motif 3#, joining on Rnd 9 to Motif #1 at one point and to Motif 2 at the next point.

Make Motif #4, joining on Rnd 5 to Motif #2 at two points and Motif #3 at two points.

Make Motif #5, joining on Rnd 6 to Motif #3 at three points and Motif #4 at two points.

Make Motif #6, joining on Rnd 8 to Motif #1 at one point and Motif #3 at one point.

Make Motif #7, joining on Rnd 4 to Motif 3 at two points and Motif #5 at two points.

Make Motif #8, joining on Rnd 5 to Motif #6 at one point, Motif #3 at one point, and Motif #7 at one point.

Make Motif #9, joining on Rnd 5 to Motif #8 at one point, Motif #7 at one point, and Motif #5 at one point.

Make Motif #1 a second time, joining on Rnd 6 to Motif #4 at two points, and Motif #5 at two points.

Make Motifs 2–9, joining as established, then make Motifs 1–9 a third time.

Edging

Attach yarn anywhere on outside edge of wrap.

Rnd 1: Work (dc, ch 4) evenly spaced into every lp around entire outside edge of wrap. Sl st to first dc.

Rnd 2: Sl st into first ch-4 sp of Rnd 1. Work (dc, ch 4) into one lp and (5 sc, ch 4) into the next. Alternate (dc, ch 4) and (5 sc, ch 4) around entire outside edge of wrap. Sl st to first dc.

Fasten off. Block to finished measurements.

Assembly Diagram

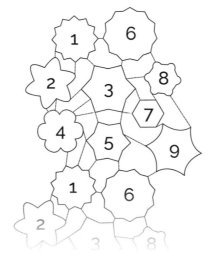

Entwined Bonnet

DESIGNED BY ANASTASIA POPOVA

The cable pattern used for this charming bonnet creates a dense, textured fabric that will keep out the chill on breezy fall and winter days. If you've never tried crochet cables, the minimal shaping in this piece is ideal for learning a more advanced post-stitch combination.

FINISHED SIZE
5¼ (6, 7, 7¾, 8½, 9¼)" [13.5 (15, 18, 19.5, 21.5, 23.5) cm] wide from front to crown and 11¼ (13, 16¾, 18½, 20¼, 22)" [28.5 (33, 42.5, 47, 51.5, 56) cm] around face opening.

Sized to fit average newborn (baby, toddler, child, teen/adult S, adult M/L). Bonnet shown in teen/adult S.

YARN
Worsted weight (#4 Medium)

Shown here: HiKoo Kenzie (50% merino, 25% nylon, 10% angora, 10% alpaca, 5% silk noils; 160 yd [146 m]/1¾ oz [50 g]): #1015, 3 skeins. Yarn distributed by Skacel Collection, Inc.

HOOK
Size 7 (4.5 mm). Adjust hook size if necessary to obtain correct gauge.

NOTIONS
Yarn needle; stitch markers.

GAUGE
20 sts and 9 rows = 4" [10 cm] in cable pattern.

3 SKEINS

STITCH GUIDE

Back Post treble crochet (BPtr): Yo twice, insert hook from back to front to back around post of corresponding st below, yo and pull up a lp [yarn over, draw through two lps] 3 times.

Back Post half treble crochet (BPhtr): Yo twice, insert hook from back to front to back around post of corresponding st below, yo and pull up a lp, yo and draw through 2 lps on hook, yo and draw through all 3 lps on hook.

Front Post half treble crochet (FPhtr): Yo twice, insert hook from front to back to front around post of corresponding st below, yo and pull up a lp, yo and draw through 2 lps on hook, yo and draw through all 3 lps on hook.

Increase Section

Row 1: Fdc 22 (26, 30, 32, 36, 40), turn.

CHILD, TEEN/ADULT S, ADULT M/L SIZES ONLY

Row 2: Ch 2 (counts as first hdc here and throughout), 2 dc in st at base of ch, [sk next 2 sts, FPtr (see Glossary) around next 2 sts, working in front of sts just made, FPtr around 2 skipped sts] across to last 3 sts, FPhtr (see Stitch Guide) around next 2 sts, dc in last st, turn—(34, 38, 42) sts.

ALL SIZES

Next row: Ch 2, [sk next 2 sts, BPtr (see Stitch Guide) around next 2 sts, working behind sts just made, BPtr around 2 skipped sts] across to last 2 sts, 2 dc in next st, dc in last st, turn—24 (28, 32, 36, 40, 44) sts.

Main Section

Row 1 (RS): Ch 2, [sk next 2 sts, FPtr around next 2 sts, working in front of sts just made, FPtr around 2 skipped sts] across to last 3 sts, FPhtr around next 2 sts, dc in last st, turn.

Row 2: Ch 2, [sk next 2 sts, BPtr around next 2 sts, working behind sts just made, BPtr around 2 skipped sts] across to last 3 sts, BPhtr (see Stitch Guide) around next 2 sts, dc in last st, turn.

Next 14 (18, 24, 26, 30, 34) rows: Rep last 2 rows.

Next row: Rep Row 1 once.

Decrease Section

Row 1: Ch 2, [sk next 2 sts, BPtr around next 2 sts, working behind sts just made, BPtr around 2 skipped sts] across to last 3 sts, dc3tog, turn—22 (26, 30, 34, 38, 42) sts.

NEWBORN, BABY, TODDLER SIZES ONLY

Row 2: Ch 2, FPdc around each st across to last st, dc in the last st—22 (26, 30) sts.

CHILD, TEEN/ADULT S, ADULT M/L SIZES ONLY

Row 2: Ch 2 (does not count as st), dc2tog in next 2 post sts, [sk next 2 sts, FPtr around next 2 sts, working in front of sts just made, FPtr around 2 skipped sts] across to last 3 sts, FPhtr around next 2 sts, dc in last st, turn—(32, 36, 40) sts.

Row 3: Ch 2, BPdc around each st across to last st, dc in the last st.

Fasten off.

Finishing

SEAMING

Using yarn tail, sew the back of the head seam; include one stitch at the bottom of the edge in seam—42 (50, 58, 62, 70, 78) sts along bottom edge.

BOTTOM EDGING

With RS facing, join yarn at the right corner of the bottom edge.

Row 1: Ch 2, [FPdc around next 2 sts, BPdc around next 2 sts] across to last st, dc in last st.

Rep Row 1 twice.

FACE OPENING

Row 1 (RS): Sc across the front edge evenly (work 2 sc for each row end).

Do not fasten off.

Tie 1: Ch 40 (44, 48, 52, 56, 60), dc in 3rd ch from hook and next ch, sc in each ch across to the bonnet.

Row 2 (RS): Rev sc (see Glossary) in each st of Row 1.

Tie 2: Rep Tie 1. Sl st into corner. Fasten off.

Weave in ends. Block lightly.

Flourish Cloche

DESIGNED BY SHARON ZIENTARA

This hat was born of my love for flapper-style cloches. I wanted something that looked fanciful and was fun and interesting to make. I first tried the ruffle element on flat, without gathering it, and it overwhelmed the hat. I loved the stitch pattern so much, though, that I tried stitching it together into a flower and I fell in love.

FINISHED SIZE
20½" in circumference × 9" tall (52 × 23 cm).

YARN
Worsted weight (#4 Medium)

Shown here: Rowan Lima (84% alpaca, 8% merino, 8% nylon; 109 yd [100 m]/1¾ oz [50 g]): #884 Cusco, 2 balls.

HOOK
Size G/6 (4 mm). Adjust hook size if necessary to obtain correct gauge.

NOTIONS
Yarn needle; stitch markers.

GAUGE
16 sts and 19 rows = 4" [10 cm] in sc rib pattern after blocking.

NOTE
Brim of hat is crocheted flat. Ruffle is worked onto one end of brim and gathered to form the ruffle. Crown of hat is then picked up from row-ends of brim.

2 SKEINS

Hat Band

Ch 83.

Row 1: (RS) Sc in 2nd ch from hook and in each ch across, turn—82 sc.

Rows 2–3: Ch 1 (does not count as st throughout), sc across, turn.

Row 4: Ch 1, sc in first sc, sc blo in each sc across to last sc, sc in last sc, turn.

Row 5: Ch 1, sc in first sc, sc flo across to last sc, sc in last sc, turn.

Rows 6-8: Rep Rows 2 and 3 , ending with Row 2.

Row 9: Rep Row 5.

Row 10: Rep Row 4.

Rows 11-13: Rep Rows 2 and 3, ending with a Row 2.

Rows 14-15: Rep Rows 4 and 5. Fasten off.

Crown

Rnd 1: With RS facing, sl st in first st of upper edge of band, ch 1 (counts as st here and throughout), sc 79 sts evenly across row to end, sl st in beg ch to join for working in the round—80 sts.

Rnd 2: Ch 1, sc in next sc, 2 sc in next sc, (sc in next 4 sc, 2 sc in next sc) 15 times, sc in last 2 sc, sl st in beg ch to join—96 sts.

Next rnd: Ch 1, sc in first sc and in each st around, sl st in first sc to join.

Rep last row until hat measures 6" (15 cm) from brim.

Next rnd: Ch 1, sc in first sc and in next 13 sc, sc2tog (see Glossary), pm in sc2tog, [sc in next 14 sc, sc2tog] 5 times, sl st in first sc to join.

Dec rnd: Ch 1, sc in first sc and in each sc to one st before marked st, sc2tog next st and marked st, [sc in each sc to one st before next m, sc2tog next st and marked st] 5 times, sl st first sc to join.

Rep Dec rnd 13 times more. Fasten off leaving a long tail to sew the top of hat closed.

Ruffle

Row 1: With WS together and working through both layers in row-ends of band, sc 20 sts evenly across row, turn—20 sts.

Row 2: Ch 4 (counts as dc, ch 1) *[dc-2tog (see Glossary) over next 2 sts, ch 1] to last st, dc in last st, turn.

Row 3: Ch 3 (counts as hdc, ch 1), 2dc-cl (see Stitch Guide) in first ch-1 sp, ch 1, *2dc-cl in next dc2tog, ch 1, 2dc-cl in next ch-1 sp, ch 1, hdc in next dc2tog, ch 1, 2dc-cl in next ch-1 sp, ch 1; rep from * 2 times, 2dc-cl in next dc2tog, ch 1, 2dc-cl in last ch-1 sp, ch 1, hdc in 3rd ch of beg ch-4, turn.

Row 4: Ch 3 (counts as hdc, ch 1) 2dc-cl in first ch-1 sp, ch 1, *[2dc-cl in next 2dc-cl, ch 1, 2dc-cl in next ch-1 sp, ch 1] 3 times, hdc in next hdc, ch 1, 2dc-cl in next ch-1 sp, ch 1; rep from *, ending last rep with hdc in 2nd ch of beg ch-3, turn.

Row 5: Ch 2, 2dc-cl in first ch-1 sp, ch 1 *[2dc-cl in next 2dc-cl, ch 1, 2dc-cl in next ch-1 sp, ch 1] 7 times, sc in hdc, ch 1, 2dc-cl in next ch-1 sp, ch 1; rep from *, ending last rep with sc in 2nd ch of beg ch-3, turn.

Row 6: Ch 1, sc in same st, [(dc, ch 2, dc) in next ch-1 sp, * (dc, ch 3, dc) in next 2dc-cl, (dc, ch 3, dc) in next ch-1 sp] 15 times, sc in next sc; rep from *, end last rep with sc in top of beg ch-2. Fasten off.

Finishing

With RS tog, whip stitch ends of Ruffle Rows 1-3 tog to form a circle. Weave in ends. Block.

Annulet Wrap

DESIGNED BY CRISTINA MERSHON

This romantic accessory gets its beautiful drape from one of my favorite fibers, alpaca. It can be worn in a multitude of ways, including over your shoulders for a special-occasion stole, or around your neck and tucked into your overcoat for extra warmth on cold days. If you prefer something less formal, just omit the beads!

FINISHED SIZE
About 60" long × 32" wide (152.5 × 81.5 cm) (main scarf only).

YARN
Sportweight (#2 Fine)

Shown here: Berroco Ultra Alpaca Fine (50% superwash wool, 30% nylon, 20% super fine alpaca; 433 yd [396 m]/3½ oz [100 g]): #12175 perwinkle mix, 3 skeins.

HOOK
Size B/1 (2.25 mm) for the ring part of the scarf; size D/3 (3.25 mm) for the body of the scarf.

NOTIONS
717 4mm beads (optional); yarn needle.

GAUGE
36 sts and 7 rows in pattern = 4" (10 cm). Gauge is not crucial.

NOTES
The scarf is constructed all in one piece, starting with the ring, which will be folded in half; ends are attached together with sc, and then continue on with the body of the scarf.

As noted in the pattern, most of the stitches on the ring are worked in the blo to create the ridge effect.

3 SKEINS

Ring

Using Size B/1 (2.25 mm) hook, ch 96, turn.

Row 1: (RS) Sl st in 2nd ch from hook and next 4 ch, [hdc next 5 ch, sl st in each of next 5 ch] across to end of row, turn—95 sts.

Note: Beg working in blo of all sts unless otherwise noted.

Row 2: Ch 1, sl st first 5 sl st, [hdc next 5 hdc, st st next 5 sl st] across to end of row, turn.

Row 3: Ch 2, hdc next 5 sl st, [sl st next 5 hdc, hdc next 5 sl st] across to end of row, turn.

Row 4: Ch 2, hdc next 5 hdc, [sl st next 5 sl st, hdc next 5 hdc] across until the end of the row, turn.

Row 5: Ch 1, sl st first 5 hdc, [hdc next 5 sl st, sl st next 5 hdc] across to end of row, turn.

Rows 6–22: Rep Rows 2–5 for pattern. At end of Row 3, do not fasten off.

JOINING

Fold the piece in half lengthwise and attach the two short ends together. Working through both layers, sc 44 evenly across to form a ring, turn. Continue working the body of the scarf.

Body of Wrap

Row 1: With Size D/3 (3.25 mm) hook, ch 3 (counts as dc), [(dc, ch 1, dc, ch 1, dc) in next sc, sk 2 sts] across to end of row, dc in last st, turn—44 dc, 28 ch-sps.

Row 2: [Ch 4, sc in next ch-1 sp] across to end of row, ch 2, hdc in last st, turn—29 ch-4 sps.

Row 3: Ch 3, (dc, ch 2, dc, ch 2, dc) in each of next ch-4 sps across to last ch-sp, dc in last ch-sp, turn—83 dc, 54 ch-sps.

Row 4: [Ch 4, sk next dc, sc in next ch-sp, ch 3, sk next dc, sc in next ch-2 sp, sk 2 dc] across to end of row, ending row with ch-2, hdc in top of turning ch, turn.

Row 5: Ch 3, sk next ch-2 sp, [(dc, ch 2, dc, ch 2, dc) in next ch-3 sp, sk next ch-4 sp] across to end of row, ending row with dc in 2nd ch of turning ch, turn.

Rows 6–114: Rep Rows 4 and 5 for pattern, turn.

Row 115: Ch 5, sk ch-2 sp, *[2 tr, picot (see Stitch Guide), 2 tr, picot, 2 tr, picot, tr in ch-3 sp, sk ch-4 sp], rep from * across to end of row, ending row with tr in 2nd ch of turning ch. Fasten off.

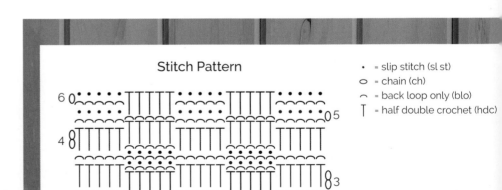

Stitch Pattern

- • = slip stitch (sl st)
- o = chain (ch)
- ⌒ = back loop only (blo)
- T = half double crochet (hdc)

Finishing

Weave in ends. Block.

The ring has a waffle texture, similar to pea pods. Sew 3 or 4 small beads to each waffle compartment (see below). On the edging, add 3 rows, or 4 or 5 beads on each shell, to meet with the picots (see photo at right).

Oblique Cowl

DESIGNED BY BETH NIELSEN

In this striking cowl, the Tunisian stitch looks deceptively like knitting, but it really is done with a hook. The fabric produced by Tunisian colorwork is thick and warm, which makes it ideal for blocking out the cold weather. The graphic pattern lends itself to all manner of color combinations, so you could easily customize the tones to men's or women's tastes.

FINISHED SIZE
11" tall × 23" in circumference (28 × 58.5 cm).

YARN
Worsted weight (#4 Medium)

Shown here: Malabrigo Worsted (100% merino wool, 210 yd [192 m]/3½ oz [100 g]): azul bolita (MC) and polar morn (CC), 1 skein each.

HOOK
Size J/10 (6 mm) double-ended Tunisian hook. Adjust hook size if necessary to obtain gauge.

NOTIONS
Yarn needle; three 1" (2.5 cm) buttons (optional).

GAUGE
18½ sts and 20½ rows = 4" (10 cm) in Tunisian Knit Stitch (tks; see Glossary).

NOTES
You can use either color to work stitches off. You'll need to use both colors for bobbins to keep the amounts even. You can even use scrap yarn for a bobbin, as you won't see the bobbin color on the outside. Always keep RS facing.

Before you start crocheting, make a bobbin with each color.

2 SKEINS

Cowl

With MC, ch 105. Join with sl st to form ring, being careful not to twist ch.

Rnd 1: Pull up a lp in each ch around, working lps off the other end of the hook as necessary, using either bobbin to work stitches off. Place marker (pm) after you pull up the last st to mark the beg of rnd. Do not turn.

Rnd 2: Working in tks in the round (see Glossary), beg colorwork according to the chart, beg with bottom right corner and working right to left, rep chart 13 times each rnd. Work the extra st at end of each rnd in MC. Do not turn or sl st to beg st, simply keep working in a spiral.

Rnds 3–41: Continue colorwork according to chart. Rep Rows 2–9 of chart 5 times. Continue to rewind and use bobbins as needed. End with a MC bobbin, as the only row the color will show in is Row 41.

Edging

Rnd 42: With MC, [sc in next st, sc2tog (see Glossary)] around, join with sl st to first sc.

Rnd 43: With CC, ch 2, hdc in same st, hdc in each sc around, join with sl st to first sc, fasten off CC.

Rnd 44: With MC, sc in each hdc around, join with sl st to first sc. Fasten off.

Work Rnds 42–44 on opposite side of foundation chain.

Fasten off.

Finishing

Weave in ends. Wet block and let dry. Sew on buttons.

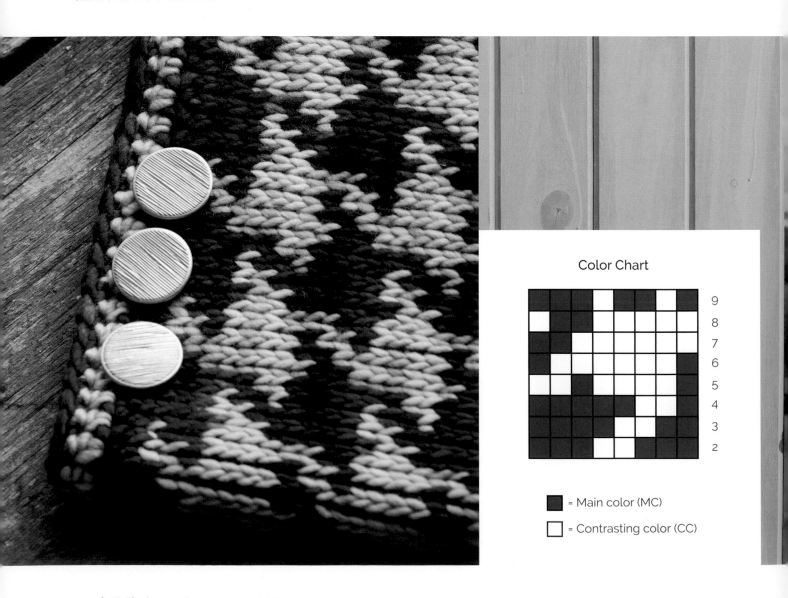

Color Chart

9
8
7
6
5
4
3
2

■ = Main color (MC)

□ = Contrasting color (CC)

Bedizened Brooch

DESIGNED BY KATHY MERRICK

Although this pretty accessory is a thread crochet project, it still works up quickly in exaggerated double crochet stitches. If you've never tried adding beads to your crochet, this is a great project to ease you into fancifying your stitches! Make several and attach them to hats, bags, or a headband.

FINISHED SIZE
Motif measures 3½" (9 cm) in diameter.

Brooch measures 8" (20.5 cm) long.

YARN
Laceweight (#0 Lace)

Shown here: DMC Pearl Cotton Thread size 8 (100% mercerized cotton; 87 yd [80 m]/.35 oz [10 g]): #606 red (CC), #524 green (MC), 1 ball each.

HOOK
Size B/1 (2.25mm).

NOTIONS
92 size 8 red glass beads (model used Beadworks beads); beading needle; metal pin back; yarn needle for attaching pin back.

GAUGE
Motif measures 3½" [9 cm] diameter. Adjust hook size if necessary to obtain gauge.

2 SKEINS

Two Double crochet cluster (2dc-cl): [Yo, insert hook in indicated st or sp, yo, draw up a loop, yo, draw through 2 loops] twice, yo, draw through 3 loops on hook.

3 Double crochet cluster (3dc-cl): [Yo, insert hook in indicated st or sp, yo, draw up a loop, yo, draw through 2 loops] 3 times, yo, draw through 4 loops on hook.

5 Double crochet cluster (5dc-cl): [Yo, insert hook in indicated st or sp, yo, draw up a loop, yo, draw through 2 loops] 5 times, yo, draw through 6 loops on hook.

Picot: Ch 1, place bead up against hook, ch 2, sl st into first ch.

Motif

Using beading needle, thread 92 beads onto MC. Make adjustable ring (see Glossary).

Rnd 1: Ch 3, 2dc-cl (see Stitch Guide) in adjustable ring, ch 3, [3dc-cl (see Stitch Guide), picot (see Stitch Guide), ch 3] 8 times in lp, sl st in top of beg st.

Rnd 2: Sl st in next ch-3 sp, ch 2, (5dc-cl [see Stitch Guide], picot, ch 5) 8 times, sl st in first 5dc-cl. Fasten off and cut MC.

Rnd 3: With CC, sl st in next ch-5 sp. *7 sc in ch-5 sp, turn, [ch 1, sc in next 7 sts, turn] 4 times; ch 4, sl st in next ch-5 sp (petal made); rep from * 7 times, ending with sl st in first sc of rnd. Fasten off CC.

Rnd 4: With MC, sl st in last sl st of Rnd 3, *sl st in each end of petal row to top of petal, sc in first sc in top row of petal, picot, sc in next 3 sts, picot, sc in next 3 sts, picot, ch 4, sl st in next ch-5 sp from Rnd 2; rep from * around ending with sl st in first sl st.

Tail

Row 1: With CC, ch 10, sl st in first ch to form ring, *ch 18, sl st in 10th ch from hook; rep from * 2 times. Ch 36, sl st in 10th ch from hook, *ch 18, sl st in 10th ch from hook; rep from * 3 times, turn.

Row 2: Ch 1, sc in each ch of tail. Break off CC.

Row 3: With MC, sl st to join in first st of Row 2, ch 1, sc in same st, sc in next st, picot, *[sc in next 3 sts, picot] 3 times, sc in next 2 sc**, sl st in each sc across to next ring, sc in next 2 sc*; rep from * to * 3 mores times, sl st in next 12 sts, [sl st in side of any Rnd two 5dc-cl on WS, sl st in next st of tail] twice, sl st to next ring of tail, sc in next 2 sts, rep between * * across, ending final rep at **. Fasten off.

Finishing

ADD PIN BACK

With yarn needle and MC, sew pin back to center back of brooch, making sure to attach securely.

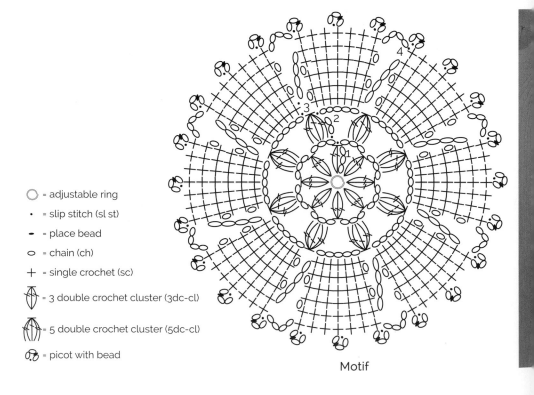

○ = adjustable ring

• = slip stitch (sl st)

‒ = place bead

○ = chain (ch)

+ = single crochet (sc)

⬮ = 3 double crochet cluster (3dc-cl)

⬮ = 5 double crochet cluster (5dc-cl)

○ᴃ = picot with bead

Motif

Stellina Hat & Fingerless Mitts

DESIGNED BY TERRI KELLER

Designer Terri Keller doesn't remember where she first learned to do the star stitch pattern, but fondly recalls making a layette set with the stitch and committing it to memory. Here, the unique texture combines with a crunchy alpaca/silk/linen blend yarn to create the perfect slouchy hat and cozy mitts.

FINISHED SIZE
Hat: 10½" long from crown to unrolled brim × 20½" in circumference (26.5 × 52 cm).

Mitts: 4" wide × 8" long (10 × 20.5 cm).

YARN
Sportweight (#2 Fine)

Shown here: HiKoo Rylie (50% baby alpaca, 25% mulberry silk, 25% linen; 274 yd [251 m]/3½ oz [100g]): color 008, 2 skeins. Yarn distributed by Skacel Collection, Inc.

HOOK
Size E/4 (3.5 mm).

NOTIONS
Stitch markers; yarn needle; ⅝" (1.5 cm) ribbon, 40" (101.5 cm) long (oftheearth.org).

GAUGE
Star Stitch Pattern—2 "stars" = 1" (2.5 cm); Solid Pattern (1 dc, 1 sc)—18 sts and 16 rows = 4" [10 cm].

2 SKEINS

STITCH GUIDE

Foundation group: Ch 1, extend lp to ¼ inch (6 mm), yo, and insert hook into st below ch-1 sp, yo, and pull up lp, while pinching the strand of working yarn with non-dominant hand, yo, draw through all 3 lps on hook, insert hook under the strand of yarn held back, yo, and draw through strand and lp on hook (sl st made), ch 1, place marker in sl st.

Turning group: Extend lp on hook by ¼ inch (6 mm) (first petal made), yo, insert hook into sl st at top of next group and pull up lp to ¼ inch (2nd petal made), pinching the strand of working yarn, yo, draw through all 3 lps on hook, insert hook under the strand of yarn held back, yo, and draw through strand and lp on hook (sl st made), ch 1.

3-petal group: Extend lp on hook by ¼ inch (6 mm) (first petal made), yo, insert hook in same sl st as last petal of prev st, yo, pull up lp by ¼ inch (2nd petal made), yo, insert hook in next sl st from row below, pull up ¼ inch lp (3rd petal made), pinching the strand of working yarn, yo, draw through all 5 lps on hook, insert hook under strand of yarn held back, yo, and draw through strand and lp on hook (sl st made), ch 1.

2-petal group: Extend lp on hook by ¼ inch (6 mm), yo, insert hook in same sl st as join, yo, pull up lp by ¼ inch (first petal made), yo, insert hook in next sl st from row below, pull up ¼ inch lp (2nd petal made), pinching the strand of working yarn, yo, draw through all 5 lps on hook, insert hook under strand of yarn held back, yo, and draw through strand and lp on hook (sl st made), ch 1.

Decrease group: Extend lp on hook by ¼ inch (6 mm), yo, insert hook in same sl st as last petal of prev st, [yo, insert hook in next sl st from row below, pull up ¼ inch lp] twice, pinching the strand of working yarn, yo, draw through all 7 lps on hook, insert hook under strand of yarn held back, yo, and draw through strand and lp on hook (sl st made), ch 1.

Solid Pattern in Rows

Row 1: Sc in 2nd ch from hook, dc in next ch [sc in next ch, dc in next ch] across, making sure to end with a dc, turn.

Row 2: Ch 1, [dc in each sc and sc in each dc] across, with dc in turning ch, turn.

Rep Row 2 for pattern.

Solid Pattern in Rounds

Ch indicated number of sts, sl st in first ch to join being careful not to twist chain.

Row 1: Ch 1, sc in same st, dc in back bump of next ch, [sc in back bump of next ch, dc in back bump of next ch] across, sl st in first ch to join.

Rnd 2: Ch 2, sc in each dc, dc in each sc around, sl st in 2nd ch to join.

Rnd 3: Ch 1, dc in each sc, sc in each dc around, sl st in first ch to join.

Fingerless Mitt (make 2)

Row 1: Work 14 foundation groups (see Stitch Guide).

Row 2: Work 3-petal group (see Stitch Guide) 13 times across, work turning group, turn.

Row 3: Work 1 turning group (see Stitch Guide), work 3-petal group 13 times across, turn.

Row 4: Work 1 foundation group, work 3-petal group 13 times, work turning group, turn.

Rows 5–8: Rep Rows 3 and 4. Do not work turning group at the end of Row 8, turn.

Row 9: Ch 1, sc in first st, work 36 stitches evenly as follows [dc, sc] across, dc in last st, turn.

Rows 10 & 11: Work Row 2 of solid pattern across.

Row 12: Work 16 sts in Row 2 of solid pattern, ch 6, sk next 6 sts, work in established solid pattern across, turn.

Row 13: Work Row 2 of solid pattern working in patt across 6 ch sts, turn.

Rows 14–26: Rep Row 2 of solid pattern. Do not turn after Row 26.

Ch 1, work 24 sc across top edge of mitt (this will be at the top of your fingers). Fasten off.

Thumb

Join yarn to skipped area to work thumb gusset, making sure the star stitch is on the top of the hand and the solid pattern is on the palm of the hand to distinguish right and left mitts. Work 16 sts in solid pattern evenly around thumb opening. Continue to work solid pattern for a total of 6 rnds. Fasten off.

Finishing

With RS tog, sew seam tog with whip-stitch (see Glossary). Weave in all ends.

Hat

Ch 96.

Work solid pattern in rnds (see Stitch Guide) for 8 rows total.

Rnd 9: Work one foundation group (see Stitch Guide) in same st as join of Rnd 8, *work 3-petal group (see Stitch Guide) with 2nd petal in same Rnd 8 st as last petal of previous group, sk 2 sts along Rnd 8, and 3rd petal in next Rnd 8 st; rep from * 31 more times, ch 1, sl st in top of first foundation group, do not turn.

Rnd 10: Work 2-petal group (see Stitch Guide) once with first petal going in same st as join, and 2nd petal in next sl st from join, work 3-petal groups around until 3rd petal of last group is worked into join, ch 1, sl st in top of first group, do not turn.

Rnds 11–24: Work one foundation group in same st as join of prev rnd, work 3-petal groups around until 3rd petal of last group is worked into join, ch 1, sl st in top of first group, do not turn.

Rnd 25: Work one foundation group in same st as join of prev rnd, work 3-petal group 3 times, [work decrease group (see Stitch Guide), work 3-petal group 6 times] 3 times, work 3-petal groups around, ch 1, sl st in top of first group, do not turn.

Rnd 26: Work one foundation group in same st as join of prev rnd, work 3-petal group 3 times, [work decrease group, work 3-petal group 5 times] 3 times, work 3-petal group once, ch 1, sl st in top of first group, do not turn.

Rnd 27: Work one foundation group in same st as join of prev rnd, work 3-petal group 3 times, [work decrease group (see Stitch Guide), work 3-petal group 4 times] 3 times, ch 1, sl st in top of first group. Fasten off.

Finishing

Cut yarn and weave through ch-1 sps around, draw tight to close. Weave in ends.

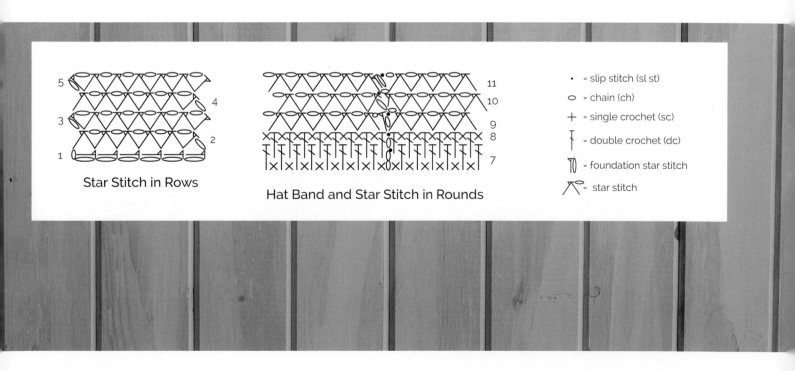

Star Stitch in Rows

Hat Band and Star Stitch in Rounds

· = slip stitch (sl st)

o = chain (ch)

+ = single crochet (sc)

┃ = double crochet (dc)

⊥ = foundation star stitch

⋏ = star stitch

Askew Scarf

DESIGNED BY SHARON ZIENTARA

I designed this scarf out of my love for anything worked on the bias. I've always thought it was such a cool, simple way to create visual interest. The painterly yarn elevates the bias effect even further. The scarf is meant as a warm-weather accessory but it could easily be modified to make a wider, cozier neck warmer.

FINISHED SIZE
3" wide × 75" long (7.5 × 191 cm).

YARN
Fingering weight (#1 Super Fine)

Shown here: Crystal Palace Yarns Mini Mochi (80% merino, 20% nylon; 195 yd [178 m]/1¾ oz [50 g]): #336 festival, 2 balls.

HOOK
Size C/2 (2.75 mm). Adjust hook size if necessary to obtain gauge.

NOTIONS
Yarn needle; blocking wires (optional); blocking pins (optional).

GAUGE
16 sc and 15 biased sc rows = 2" (5 cm).

2 SKEINS

Scarf

Ch 31.

Row 1: Sc in bottom bump of 2nd ch from hook and in each ch across, turn—30 sts.

Row 2: Ch 1, 2 sc blo in first sc, sc blo in each sc across to last 2 sc, sc2tog (see Glossary) in blo of last 2 sc, turn.

Row 3: Ch 1, sc in each sc across, turn.

Rep Rows 2 and 3 until piece measures 6" (15 cm).

Next row: Ch 2 (does not count as st), 2 hdc blo in first st, [ch 1, sk next st, hdc blo in next st] across to last 3 sts, ch 1, sk next st, hdc2tog (see Glossary) in blo of last 2 sts, turn.

Next row: Ch 2 (does not count as st), hdc in each st across, turn.

Rep last 2 rows until scarf measures 69" (175 cm).

Rep Rows 2 and 3 until scarf end measures 6" (15 cm). Fasten off. Weave in ends.

Finishing

Block scarf heavily with WS facing up in order to counteract any curling on the edges. I recommend using blocking wires, but a generous amount of pins will also work.

Floret Cloche

DESIGNED BY JESSICA BOLOF

This fun-to-stitch hat gets its unique construction from one of designer Jessica Bolof's first crochet projects: a dishcloth pattern her great aunt Dolores loved to make by the dozen to give away as gifts. Since only a wee bit of the contrasting colors of yarn is used to create the flower, you could easily make several hats by simply rotating the color that's used for the main body and the embellishments.

FINISHED SIZE
19" in circumference × 7½" deep (48.5 × 19 cm).

YARN
DK weight (#3 Light)

Shown here: HiKoo Simplicity (55% merino superwash, 28% acrylic, 17% nylon, 117 yd [107 m]/1¾ oz [50 g]): #25 mint (A), #24 blueberry (B), #33 red hat purple (C), 1 skein each. Yarn distributed by Skacel Collection, Inc.

HOOK
Size I/9 (5.5 mm)

GAUGE
18 dc and 8 dc rows = 4" [10 cm].

NOTES
This hat is worked beginning at the flower leaves and crocheted outward. It's shaped down the back without any seams before working the flower and hat edging.

Turning chs are not included in st counts.

3 SKEINS

STITCH GUIDE

Two treble cluster (2tr-cl): *Yo twice, insert hook in indicated st/sp, yo, and pull up loop, [yo, draw through 2 loops] twice; rep from * once, yo, draw through all loops on hook.

Three treble cluster (3tr-cl): *Yo twice, insert hook in indicated st/sp, yo, and pull up loop, [yo, draw through 2 loops] twice; rep from * twice, yo, draw through all loops on hook.

Split double crochet four together (spdc4tog): Yo, insert hook in same ch-sp as last st made, yo, and pull up loop, yo, draw through 2 loops on hook, [yo, insert hook in next ch-sp, yo, and pull up loop, yo, draw through 2 loops on hook] 3 times, yo, draw through all 5 loops on hook.

Double crochet 7 together (dc7tog): Yo, insert hook in next stitch, yo and pull up lp, yo and draw through 2 lps] 7 times, yo, draw through all lps on hook—6 sts decreased.

Flower Leaves

With A ch 5, sl st in first ch to join rnd.

Rnd 1: Ch 3, sc in first ch, (ch 2, sc in next ch) 3 more times, ch 2, sl st in first ch of beg ch-3 to join—5 sc, 5 ch-2 sps.

Rnd 2: Ch 4, sc in next sc, (ch 3, sc in next sc) 3 more times, ch 3, sl st in first ch of beg ch-4 to join—5 sc, 5 ch-3 sps.

Rnd 3: Ch 5, sc in next sc, (ch 4, sc in next sc) 3 more times, ch 4, sl st in first ch of beg ch-5 to join—5 sc, 5 ch-4 sps.

Rnd 4: Ch 3, sc in next ch-sp, ch 2, [sc in next sc, ch 2, sc in middle of ch-sp, ch 2] 4 times, sl st in first ch of beg ch-3 to join—10 sc, 10 ch-2 sps.

Rnd 5: Ch 3, 2tr-cl (see Stitch Guide) in next ch-sp, ch 4, [3tr-cl (see Stitch Guide) in next ch-sp, ch 4] 9 times. With B, sl st to join in top of beg ch-3—10 cl, 10 ch-sps.

Hat Body

Beg working in turned rows.

Row 1: (RS) Ch 3, (3 dc, ch 2, 3 dc) in each ch-sp around, sl st in first ch of beg ch-3 to join, turn—60 dc, 10 ch-2 sps.

Row 2: (WS) Ch 4, [3 dc in next ch-sp, ch 2, sk 3 dc, 3 dc in sp between groups of 3-dc, ch 2] 6 times, dc in next ch-sp, turn—40 dc.

Row 3: (RS) Ch 2, [(3 dc, ch 2) in next ch-sp] 13 times, 3 dc in last ch-4 sp, turn—42 dc.

Row 4: Ch 4, [(3 dc, ch 2) in each ch-sp] 13 times, ch 2, dc in turning ch, turn—40 dc.

Row 5: Ch 2, [(3 dc, ch 2) in next ch-sp] 5 times, [2 dc in next ch-sp, spdc4tog (see Stitch Guide), ch 2] twice, [(3 dc, ch 2) in next ch-sp] 4 times, 3 dc in last ch-4 sp, turn—36 sts, 11 ch-2 sps.

Row 6: Ch 4, [(3 dc, ch 2) in next ch-sp] 4 times, [2 dc in next ch-sp, spdc4tog, ch 2] twice, [(3 dc, ch 2) in next ch-sp] 3 times, dc in top of turning ch, turn—23 sts, 10 ch-sps.

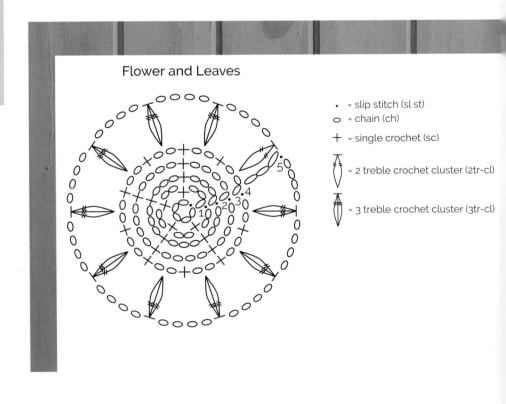

Flower and Leaves

- • = slip stitch (sl st)
- ○ = chain (ch)
- + = single crochet (sc)
- = 2 treble crochet cluster (2tr-cl)
- = 3 treble crochet cluster (3tr-cl)

Row 7: Ch 2, [(3 dc, ch 2) in next ch-sp 2] 3 times, 2 dc in next ch-sp, dc7tog (see Stitch Guide) with first leg in current ch-sp, next 3 legs in next ch-sp and last 3 legs in following ch-sp, ch 2, [(3 dc, ch 2) in next ch-sp] 3 times, 3 dc in ch-4 sp, turn—24 sts, 7 ch-2 sps.

Row 8: Ch 4, [(3 dc, ch 2) in next ch-sp] 3 times, 2 dc in next ch-sp, spdc4tog, ch 2, [(3 dc, ch 2) in next ch-sp] twice, dc in top of turning ch, turn—19 sts, 7 ch-sps.

Row 9: Ch 2, [(3 dc, ch 2) in next ch-sp] twice, 2 dc in next ch-sp, spdc4tog, ch 2, [(3 dc, ch 2) in next ch-sp] twice, 3 dc in ch-4 sp, turn—18 sts, 5 ch-2 sps.

Row 10: Ch 4, 3 dc in next ch-sp, ch 2, [2 dc in next ch-sp, spdc4tog, ch 2] twice, dc in top of turning ch, turn—10 sts, 4 ch-sps.

Row 11: Ch 2, 2 dc in first ch-sp, (dc-7tog with first leg in current ch-sp, next 3 legs in next ch-sp and last 3 legs in next ch-sp, ch 2, 3 dc in ch-4 sp, turn— 6 sts.

Row 12: Ch 2, sk all sts from prev rnd, sl st in top of turning ch.

Do not fasten off.

Edging

Beg working in rnds.

Rnd 1: With RS facing, ch 1, (sc, 5 dc) in last ch-2 sp made in Row 12, [(sc, 5 dc) in next ch-sp] 5 times, [(sc, dc, sc) in between next 2 pairs of 3-dc groups, (sc, 5 dc) in next ch-sp] 4 times, [(sc, 5 dc) in next ch-sp] 4 times, sl st in first ch to join—96 sts. Fasten off.

Flower

Flower is worked in spiral rnds. Work each petal around the ch-sp in between sc of flower leaves.

With C and RS of hat facing, join with sl st in center ring between any two sc.

Rnd 1: Ch 1, [(sc, dc, sc) in each ch-sp of center ring] around—15 sts.

Rnd 2: [(Sc, 2 dc, sc) in each ch-sp of Leaves Rnd 2] around—20 sts.

Rnd 3: [(Sc, 3 dc, sc) in each ch-sp of Leaves Rnd 3] around—25 sts.

Rnd 4: [(Sc, 2 dc) in next ch-sp, (2 dc, sc) in next ch-sp] around—30 sts.

Fasten off.

Finishing

Weave in ends. Block to measurements.

Garland Wrap

DESIGNED BY KATHY MERRICK

This motif wrap takes a Japanese-inspired stitch pattern to a new level. The exploded flowers and long chain strands make for an eye-catching and fun-to-stitch accessory. Like many projects in this collection, this design lends itself to myriad color combinations. Just pick your favorite flower, find yarn colors to match, and crochet this beautiful, everlasting bouquet.

FINISHED SIZE
92" long × 16" wide (234 × 40.5 cm) after blocking.

YARN
Fingering weight (#1 Super Fine)

Shown here: Madelinetosh Tosh Merino Light (100% merino wool; 420 yd [384 m]/3½ oz [100 g]): Betty Draper's blues (MC), magenta (CC), 1 skein each.

HOOK
Size E/4 (3.5 mm). Adjust hook size if necessary to obtain gauge.

NOTIONS
Stitch markers.

GAUGE
Large chain motif = 5¼" (13.5 cm) diameter after blocking.

Small flower = 2" (5 cm) diameter after blocking.

2 SKEINS

Large Chain Motif

With MC, ch 7; join with sl st to form ring.

Rnd 1: Ch 1, 12 sc in ring, sl st in first sc of rnd—12 sc.

Rnd 2: Ch 1, 2 sc in each sc of previous rnd, sl st in first sc of rnd—24 sc.

Rnd 3: Ch 1, [sc in next sc, ch 20, place marker (pm) in 10th ch] 5 times, [sc in next sc, ch 20] 3 times, [sc in next sc, ch 20, pm in 10th ch] twice, [sc in next sc, ch 20] 14 times, sl st in first sc of rnd to join. Fasten off.

Adjacent Chain Motif A

Work to end of Rnd 2 of Large Chain Motif. Find 5 consecutive marked ch-20 lps on previous motif.

Rnd 3: Ch 1, [sc in next sc of current motif, ch 10, sc in first marked ch-20 lp of previous Large Chain Motif, ch 10] 5 times, [sc in next sc of current motif, ch 20] 8 times, [sc in next sc of current motif, ch 20, pm in 10th ch] 5 times, [sc in next sc of current motif, ch 20] 6 times, sl st in first sc of rnd to join. Fasten off.

First Small Flower Motif

With CC, ch 10; join with sl st to form ring.

Rnd 1: Ch 1, 24 sc in ring, sl st in first sc of rnd—24 sc.

Rnd 2: Ch 3 (counts as first dc), dc in next 2 sts, ch 1, sc in first marked ch-20 lp of first Large Chain Motif, ch 1, dc in next 3 sts of current motif, ch 1, sc in in next marked ch-20 lp of first Large Chain Motif, ch 1, [dc in next 3 sts of current motif, ch 3] 6 times, (pm in first and 2nd ch-3 sps just made), sl st in top of beg ch-3 sp. Fasten off.

Assembly Diagram

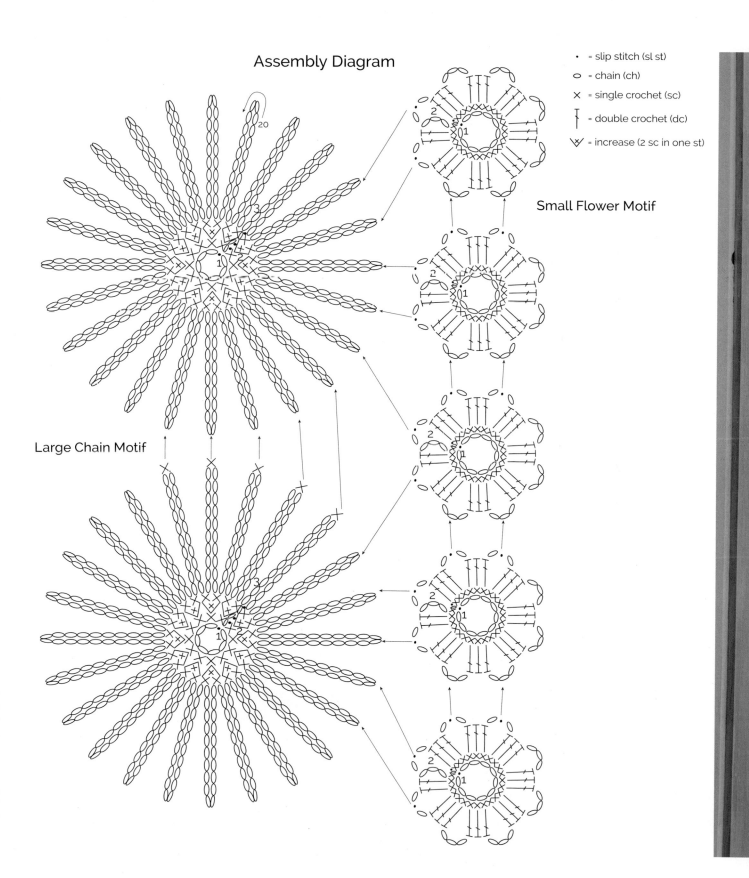

= slip stitch (sl st)

= chain (ch)

= single crochet (sc)

= double crochet (dc)

= increase (2 sc in one st)

Small Flower Motif

Large Chain Motif

Second Small Flower Motif

Rnd 1: Rep Rnd 1 of First Small Flower Motif.

Rnd 2: Ch 3 (counts as first dc), dc in next 2 sts, [ch 1, sc in marked ch-3 sp of previous Small Flower Motif, ch 1, dc in next 3 sts of current motif] twice, [ch 1, sc in next ch-20 lps of adjacent Large Chain Motif, ch 1, dc in next 3 sts of current motif] twice, ch 3, [dc in next 3 sts, ch 3] 3 times, (pm in first and 2nd ch-3 sps just made), sl st in top of beg ch-3 sp. Fasten off.

Third Small Flower Motif

Rnd 1: Rep Rnd 1 of First Small Flower Motif.

Rnd 2: Ch 3 (counts as first dc), dc in next 2 sts, [ch 1, sc in marked ch-3 sp of previous Small Flower Motif, ch 1, dc in next 3 sts of current motif] twice, ch 1, sc in next 2 ch-20 lps of adjacent Large Chain Motif, ch 1, dc in next 3 sts of current motif, ch 1, sc in first available ch-20 lp of next adjacent Large Chain Motif, ch 1, [dc in next 3 sts, ch 3] 4 times, (pm in 2nd and 3rd ch-3 sps just made), sl st in top of beg ch-3 sp. Fasten off.

Fourth Small Flower Motif

Rep Second Small Flower Motif.

Wrap

RIGHT SECTION

Make first Large Chain Motif.

Work adjacent Large Chain Motif A 14 times.

MIDDLE SECTION

With CC, make First Small Flower Motif.

[Work Second Small Flower Motif, work Third Small Flower Motif, work Fourth Small Flower Motif] 14 times, work Second Small Flower Motif once more.

LEFT SECTION

With MC, work Large Chain Motifs as for right section, reversing joining positions.

EDGING

Rnd 1: With CC, beg in any outside lp and work ([sc, ch 3, sc], ch 3) in each ch-lp around wrap, ending with sl st to first sc at beg of rnd.

Rnd 2: Sl st in first ch-3 sp of Rnd 1, ch 1, (sc, ch 5, sc) in same ch sp, ch 5, sk next ch-3 sp, *(sc, ch 5, sc) in next ch-3 sp, ch 5, sk next ch-3 sp; rep from * around, ending with sl st in first sc. Fasten off.

Wet block wrap to finished measurements.

Engild Mitts

DESIGNED BY LINDA SKUJA

Linda Skuja's first real crochet project (besides a swatch that she turned into a potholder) was a sideways pair of fingerless mitts, and she wore them often. This lacy pair is quick to make, even for an inexperienced crocheter. The open stitch pattern lightens up the look and makes this an accessory you can show off in almost any season.

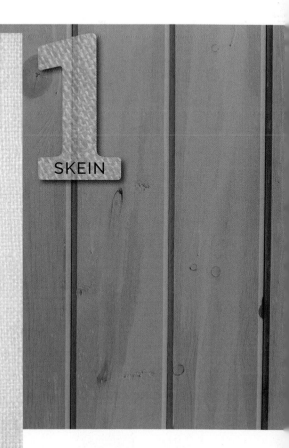

FINISHED SIZE
Each mitt is 3¾" wide × 8¼" long (9.5 × 21 cm).

One size fits most.

YARN
Sportweight (#2 Fine)

Shown here: Cascade Yarns 220 Superwash Sport (100% merino; 136 yd [124 m]/1¾ oz [50 g]): #882 plum crazy, 1 skein.

HOOKS
Size G/6 (4 mm) for size S mitts; Size 7 (4.5 mm) for size M/L mitts. Adjust hook size if necessary to obtain correct gauge.

NOTIONS
Stitch markers; yarn needle.

GAUGE
16 sts and 11 rows = 4" (10 cm) in dc with size G/6 (4 mm) hook.

17 sts and 9 rows = 4" (10 cm) in dc with size 7 (4.5 mm) hook.

NOTE
Each mitt is worked sideways, and the thumbs are attached afterwards.

1 SKEIN

Mitt

Ch 48.

Row 1: (Place marker [pm] in 6th ch from hook), sc in 9th ch from hook (counts as 3 skipped ch, 1 dc and ch 2), [ch 5, sk next 4 ch, sc in next ch, pm in sc just made] 7 times, ch 2, sk next 3 ch, dc in last ch (pm in last dc made), turn.

Row 2 (WS): Ch 3 (counts as first dc here and throughout), 3 dc in next ch-2 sp, ch 2, sc in next ch-5 sp, ch 2, [(3 dc, ch 2) twice in next ch-5 sp, sc in next ch-5 sp, ch 2] 3 times, 3 dc in last ch-2 sp, dc 3rd ch from marked ch, turn.

Row 3: Ch 1, sc in first dc, ch 3, dc in next 3 dc, sk next (ch-2 sp, sc, ch-2 sp), dc in next 3 dc, ch 3, [sc in next ch-2 sp, ch 3, dc in next 3 dc, sk next (ch-2 sp, sc, ch-2 sp), dc in next 3 dc, ch 3] 3 times, sc in last dc, turn.

Row 4: Ch 5 (counts as dc and ch 2), sk next ch-3 sp, sc in next dc, ch 5, sk 4 dc, sc in next dc, [ch 5, sk next (ch-3 sp, sc, ch-3 sp), sc in next dc, ch 5, sk 4 dc, sc in next dc] 3 times, ch 2, sk next ch-3 sp, dc in last sc, turn.

Row 5: Ch 1, sc in first dc, ch 2, sk next ch-2 sp, (3 dc, ch 2) twice in next ch-5 sp, [sc in next ch-5 sp, ch 2, (3 dc, ch 2) twice in next ch-5 sp] 3 times. Sc in last dc, turn.

Row 6: Ch 3, sk next ch-2 sp, dc in next 3 dc, ch 3, sc in next ch-2 sp, ch 3, dc in next 3 dc, [sk next (ch-2 sp, sc, ch-2 sp), dc in next 3 dc, ch 3, sc in next ch-2 sp, ch 3, dc in next 3 dc] 3 times, sk next ch-2 sp, dc in last sc, turn.

Row 7: Ch 5 (counts as dc and ch 2), sk first 3 dc, sc in next dc, ch 5, sk next (ch-3 sp, sc, ch-3 sp), sc in next dc, [ch 5, sk 4 dc, sc in next dc, ch 5, sk next (ch-3 sp, sc, ch-3 sp), sc in next dc] 3 times, ch 2, sk next 2 dc, dc in last dc, turn. For Right Hand, pm in 2nd to last ch-5 sp.

Rows 8–13: Rep Rows 2–7. For Left Hand, pm in 2nd from beg ch-5 sp.

Rows 14 and 15: Rep Rows 2 and 3.

Joining row 16: Fold piece in half lengthwise, with RS tog, ch 3, sc in first marked stitch, ch 2, sk next ch-3 sp, work sc through both layers, inserting hook through next dc and next marked sc from Row 1, [ch 2, sk 4 dc, sc around next ch-5 from Row 1, ch 2, work sc through both layers, inserting hook through next dc and next marked sc from Row 1, ch 2, sk next (ch-3 sp, sc, ch-3 sp), sc around next ch-5 from Row 1, ch 2, work sc through both layers, inserting hook through next dc and next marked sc from Row 1] 3 times, ch 2, sk 4 dc, sc around next ch-5 from Row 1, ch 2, work sc through both layers, inserting hook through next dc and next marked sc from Row 1, ch 2, sk next ch-3 sp, yo, draw through marked st from Row 1, yo, pull through 3 lps on hook. Fasten off. Turn RS out.

Fold piece so seam lies in center and lands on palm of hand. The marked ch-5 hole from Row 13 (for Right Hand) and Row 7 (for Left Hand) is the thumb hole. Stretch it larger.

Thumb

Rnd 1: With RS facing, and thumb opening facing you, sl st to join in st at narrow end of ch-5 sp thumb opening, ch 4 (counts as dc and ch 1), work [dc, ch 1] 11 times clockwise and evenly around opening, join with sl st to top of beg ch-3.

Rnd 2: Ch 3, [dc in next ch-1 sp, dc in next dc] 7 times, dc in next ch-1 sp, join with sl st to first dc.

Rnd 3: Ch 3, dc in next 2 dc, dc2tog in next 2 dc, [dc in next 3 dc, dc2tog in next 2 dc] twice, dc in next dc, join with sl st to first dc.

Fasten off. Weave in ends.

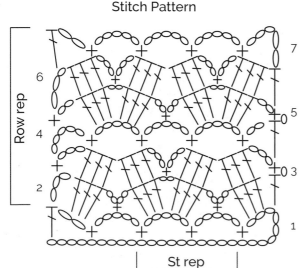

Stitch Pattern

o = chain (ch)

+ = single crochet (sc)

┬ = double crochet (dc)

Row rep

St rep

Tessellation Socks

DESIGNED BY ANASTASIA POPOVA

These cozy socks are a thoughtful hybrid of Tunisian crochet and regular crochet. Working the body of the sock in Tunisian crochet makes for a comfortable fit. And since it's worked in spiral strips around, you don't even need a Tunisian hook! The strips combine with the variegated yarn to create a subtle tiled pattern.

FINISHED SIZE
6¾" (7¾, 8¾)" [17 (19.5, 22) cm] foot circumference to fit S-6 (M-7/8, L-9/10) Women's shoe size.

YARN
Fingering weight (#1 Super Fine)

Shown here: Malabrigo Sock (100% superwash merino wool; 440 yd [402 m]/3½ oz [100 g]): #802 terracota, 1 (1, 2) skeins.

HOOK
Size E/4 (3.5 mm); D/3 (3.25 mm). Adjust hook size if necessary to obtain correct gauge.

NOTIONS
Stitch markers; yarn needle.

GAUGE
18 sts = 3" (7.5 cm) and 4 rows = 3¼" (8.5 cm) with bigger hook in tessellation st pattern, 14 ssc and 15 sc rows = 2" (5 cm) with smaller hook.

NOTE
The sock is worked from the toe up with an afterthought heel.

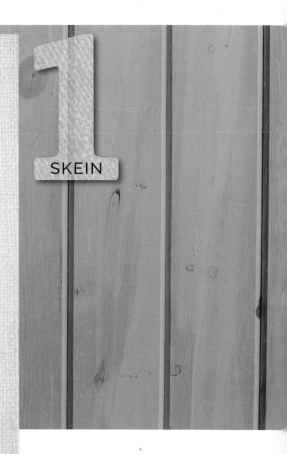

1 SKEIN

Foundation Honeycomb Stitch 1 (FHST1): Sk first vertical bar, [tps in next vertical bar, tss (see Glossary) in next vertical bar] twice, insert hook in the final vertical bar and the horizontal thread right behind it, yo, and pull up lp. Return Pass (RetP) (see Glossary).

Foundation Honeycomb Stitch 2 (FHST2): Sk first vertical bar, [tss in next vertical bar, tps in next vertical bar] twice, insert hook in the final vertical bar and the horizontal thread right behind it, yo, pull up lp. RetP as for tss.

Honeycomb Stitch 1 (HST1): Sk first vertical bar, [tps (see Glossary) in next vertical bar, tss (see Glossary) in next vertical bar] twice, insert hook in next st, yo, pull up lp—6 lps on hook. [Yo, pull through 2 lps] 5 times.

Honeycomb Stitch 2 (HST2): Sk first vertical bar, [tss in next vertical bar, tps in next vertical bar] twice, insert hook in next st, yo, pull up lp—6 lps on hook. [Yo, pull through 2 lps] 5 times.

Honeycomb Stitch Gauge Swatch

Row 1: With size E/4 (3.5 mm) hook, ch 6; insert hook in 2nd ch from hook, yo, pull up lp; [insert hook in next ch, yo, pull up lp] across to end of ch leaving all lps on the hook. RetP as for tss; FHST once, [FHST2 once, FHST1 once] 8 times.

Row 2: Ch 6, pull up lp in 2nd ch from hook and in next 3 ch, insert hook in st at base of ch, yo, pull up lp (6 lps on hook); [yo, pull through 2 lps] 5 times, HST1 in next st, [HST2 in next st, HST1 in next st] across.

Rep Row 2 two more times.

Blocked piece measures 3" (7.5 cm) wide and 3¼" (8.5 cm) long.

Toe

With smaller hook, ch 10 (11, 12).

Rnd 1: 2 sc in 2nd ch from hook, sc in each ch across to last ch, 3 sc in last ch, rotate work to work across opposite side of starting ch, sc in next 8 (9, 10) ch—20 (22, 24) sts.

Rnd 2: 3 sc in next st (place marker [pm] in middle st of 3 just made), sc in next 9 (10, 11) sts, 3 sc in next st (pm in middle st), sc in rem sts—24 (26, 28) sts.

Rnd 3: Sc in each st to m, 3 sc in marked st (move m up)] twice, sc in rem sts—28 (30, 32) sts.

Rep Rnd 3 three (four, five) more times—40 (46, 52) sts.

Next rnd: Sc in each st around.

Rep last rnd 5 more times.

Foot

In the next row, the spiral honeycomb pattern is set up.

Rnd 1: Sc in next st. Inserting hook in side vertical strand of st just made, yo, pull up lp, insert hook in next st of toe, yo, pull up lp (3 lps on hook), [yo, pull through 2 lps] twice. Tss in first vertical bar of st just made, tps in next vertical bar, insert hook in next st of toe, yo, pull up lp (4 lps on hook), [yo, pull through 2 lps] 3 times. Tss in first vertical bar, tps in next vertical bar, tss in next vertical bar, insert hook in next st of toe, yo, pull up lp (5 lps on hook), [yo, pull through 2 lps] 4 times. Tss in first vertical bar, tps in next vertical bar, tss in next vertical bar, tps in next vertical bar, insert hook in next st of toe, yo, pull up lp (6 lps on hook), [yo, pull through 2 lps] 5 times. HST1 in next st, [HST2 in next st, HST1 in next st] around.

Rnd 2: [HST2 in next, HST1 in next st] around.

Rep Rnd 2 one (two, three) more times.

Gusset

Gusset increases will be made on each side of the foot in next 2 rnds.

Rnd 1: [HST2 in next st, HST1 in next st] 4 (5, 6) times, HST2 in next st, (HST1, HST2) in next st, [HST1 in next st, HST2 in next st] 10 (11, 12) times, (HST1, HST2) in next st, [HST1 in next st, HST2 in next st] across—42 (48, 54) sts.

Rnd 2: [HST2 in next st, HST1 in next st] 5 (6, 7) times, (HST2, HST1) in next st, [HST2 in next st, HST1 in next st] 11 (12, 13) times, HST2 in next st, (HST1, HST2) in next st, [HST1 in next st, HST2 in next st] across—44 (50, 56) sts.

Heel Opening

In next 2 rnds, heel opening will be created. Heel opening will actually include some sts in Rnd 1 and some sts in Rnd 2. It is done in this way so the beginning of the spiral and the end are not visible from the top of the foot.

Rnds 1 & 2: [HST2 in next st, HST1 in next st] 18 (21, 24) times, [FHST2 in next st, FHST1 in next st] 11 times, sk next 23 sts of sock. With next st join piece to the sock as follows: Work as for FHST2 until 5 lps are formed, insert hook in last vertical bar and next st of the sock, yo, pull up lp, [yo, pull through 2 loops] 5 times, [HST1 in next st, HST2 in next st] across.

Leg

Rnd 1: [HST2 in next st, HST1 in next st] around.

Rep Rnd 1 one (two, three) more times.

Cuff

Cuff is worked sideways. Ch 10.

Row 1: Hdc in 3rd ch from hook and each ch across, sk next st of sock, sl st in next 2 sts of the sock—8 hdc.

Row 2: Turn, sl st blo in each hdc across—8 sl sts.

Row 3: Ch 1 loosely, turn, hdc blo in each st across, sk next st of sock, sl st in next 2 sts of the sock—8 hdc.

Rep Rows 2 and 3 around the leg. Fasten off leaving 7" (18 cm) long tail.

Heel

Heel is worked in continuous rnds. First rnd is worked in the heel opening, extra stitch is made at each corner, pm to mark those places.

With smaller hook, join anywhere at the heel opening.

Rnd 1: [Sc in each st to m, sc in marked st (move m up)] twice, sc in rem sts—44 (48, 52) sts.

Rnd 2: [Sc in each st to 1 st before m, sc2tog (see Glossary) (move m up)] twice, sc in rem sts—42 (46, 50) sts.

Rnd 3: [Sc in each st to m, sc2tog] twice, sc in rem sts—40 (44, 48) sts.

Rep Rnd 3 until 24 sts remain.

Last rnd: [Sc2tog in next st, sc in next st] around—16 sts.

Fasten off leaving 7" (18 cm) long tail.

Finishing

With yarn needle and yarn tail, sew the sides of the cuff together. With WS facing, flatten edge of the heel opening to align sts. With yarn needle, seam the opening using the mattress stitch.

Zaftig Mittens

DESIGNED BY BRENDA K. B. ANDERSON

These chunky mittens feature a linked double crochet stitch pattern that minimizes the open spaces between stitches and creates a warmer fabric. The bulky yarn means this project whips up in no time, and the no-frills design makes it perfect for men, women, and kids.

FINISHED SIZE
Mitten pattern is sized for Women's S, Women's M, Women's L/ Men's S, and Men's M.

About 10 (10½, 11, 11¾)" (25.5 [26.5, 28, 30] cm) from wrist edge to fingertip and about 8½ (9, 9½, 9¾)" (21.5 [23, 24, 25] cm) in circumference, not including thumb.

YARN
Chunky weight (#5 Bulky)

Shown here: Brown Sheep Lamb's Pride Bulky (85% wool, 15% mohair; 125 yd [114 m]/4 oz [113 g]): #VM245 dreamy nite, 2 skeins.

HOOK
Size I/9 (5.5 mm). Adjust hook size if necessary to obtain correct gauge.

NOTIONS
Stitch marker; yarn needle.

GAUGE
12 ldc blo sts = 4" (10 cm) and 7 rounds of ldc blo = 4¼" (11 cm).

NOTES
This mitten is worked at a tight gauge in order to minimize the gaps between rows. The linked stitches are made into the back lps of previous rounds, allowing the fabric to be flexible even though it is worked at such a tight gauge.

The mitten is made in the round without joins from the bottom up.

When weaving in ends, twist yarn (in the same direction as it was already twisted) to strengthen it.

2 SKEINS

Linked double crochet through back loop only (ldc blo):

To make a ldc blo when previous st is a dc, insert hook from right to left through the middle of the post of the previous dc st (**figure 1**), yo, and pull through just this lp (2 lps now on hook), insert hook under the back lp only of next st, yo, and pull through to front of work (3 lps now on hook; **figure 2**), [yo, and pull through 2 lps] twice (1 ldc made). To make a ldc blo when previous st is a ldc, insert hook from top to bottom under the center horizontal strand across the post of the previous ldc st, yo, and pull through just this lp (2 lps now on hook), insert hook under the back lp only of the next st, yo, and pull through to front of work (3 lps now on hook), [yo, and pull through 2 lps] twice (1 ldc made).

Linked double crochet/ single crochet increase (ldc/ sc inc):

Ldc blo in next st, insert hook from top to bottom under horizontal strand of ldc you just made, yo, and pull up lp, yo, and pull through both lps on hook to make a sc st.

Note: On the following linked st, you will insert hook under the same horizontal strand that you just worked into.

Linked double crochet two stitches together working through the back lps only (ldc2tog blo):

This is a decrease st. Insert hook from top to bottom through horizontal strand of previous linked dc st, yo, and draw up lp (2 lps now on hook), insert hook under the back lp of next st, then insert hook under the back lp of the following stitch, yo, and draw lp through both stitches (3 lps now on hook), yo, and pull through two lps on hook, yo, and pull through 2 remaining lps on hook—this reduces your stitch count by 1 stitch.

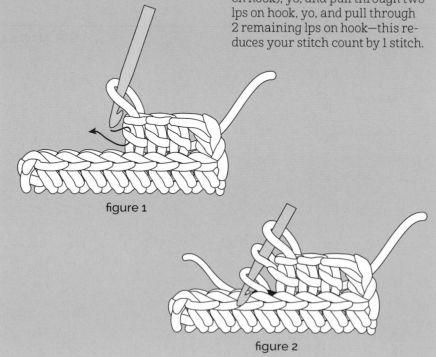

figure 1

figure 2

Mitten (make 2)

Ch 24 (25, 27, 28).

Row 1: Starting with the 2nd ch from hook and working into the bottom bar (bump) of the chain, sc blo in the next st (place st marker in this sc st), hdc blo in the next st, dc blo in the next st, ldc blo (see Stitch Guide) in each of the next 20 (21, 23, 24) sts—23 (24, 26, 27) sts.

Note: The first st of the next rnd will be made in the first st of this row (the sc st). From this point on, work in the rnd without joining.

Rnd 2: Being careful not to twist ch, and beg with marked st, ldc blo in each st around.

Note: On the first ldc of this rnd, you will be inserting your hook under the horizontal strand of the last stitch of the previous rnd.

Rnds 3–5: Ldc blo in each st.

Rnd 6: [Ldc/sc inc (see Stitch Guide)] twice, 1 ldc blo in each of the remaining 21 (22, 24, 25) sts—25 (26, 28, 29) sts.

Rnd 7: 1 ldc blo in the next st, [ldc/ sc inc] twice, 1 ldc blo in each of the remaining 22 (23, 25, 26) sts—27 (28, 30, 31) sts.

Rnd 8: 1 ldc blo in each of the next 2 sts, [ldc/sc inc] twice, 1 ldc blo in each of the remaining 23 (24, 26, 27) sts—29 (30, 32, 33) sts.

Rnd 9: 1 ldc blo in each of the next 3 sts, [ldc/sc inc] twice, 1 ldc blo in each of the remaining 24 (25, 27, 28) sts—31 (32, 34, 35) sts.

SIZE WOMEN'S S ONLY

Sk Rnd 10 and go to Rnd 11 directly.

ALL OTHER SIZES

Rnd 10: 1 ldc blo in each of the next 4 sts, [ldc/sc inc] twice, 1 ldc blo in each of the remaining (26, 28, 29) sts—(34, 36, 37) sts.

ALL SIZES

Rnd 11: Ldc/sc inc, sk each of the next 9 (10, 10, 10) sts for thumb, ldc/sc inc in following st (don't forget to link this to the horizontal strand of the previous stitch), 1 ldc blo in each of the next 20 (22, 24, 25) sts—24 (26, 28, 29) sts, not including thumb. Place marker (pm) in first skipped st.

Rnds 12–16 (12–16, 12–17, 12–18): 1 ldc blo in each st—24 (26, 28, 29) sts.

Rnd 17 (17, 18, 19): Ldc2tog blo (see Stitch Guide) 12 (13, 14, 14) times, ldc blo in the next 0 (0, 0, 1) sts—12 (13, 14, 15) sts.

Rnd 18 (18, 19, 20): Insert hook from top to bottom under horizontal strand of previous st, yo, and pull through lp (2 lps on hook), insert hook under back lp of next st, yo, and pull through to front of work (3 lps on hook), yo, and pull through all three lps, sc2tog blo 5 (6, 6, 7) times, sc blo in the next 1 (0, 1, 0) sts—6 (6, 7, 7) sts.

Fasten off. Using yarn needle, weave yarn tail through the front lp of each remaining st. Pull tight to close top of mitten and weave in end.

Thumb

Rnd 1: Leave long beg yarn tail on outside of work. With WS facing, join yarn by pulling up a lp through the blo of marked st, ch 1, sc blo in same st, dc blo in next st, ldc blo in each of the next 7 (8, 8, 8) sts, make 4 ldc sts across the gap (where thumb meets hand), do not join—11 (12, 12, 12) sts.

Rnd 2: Ldc blo in each of the next 9 (10, 10, 10) sts, [ldc2tog blo] twice—11 (12, 12, 12) sts.

Rnd 3: Ldc blo in each of the next 7 (8, 8, 10) sts, [ldc2tog blo] twice (twice, twice, once)—9 (10, 10, 11) sts.

SIZE MEN'S M ONLY
Rnd 4: 1 ldc blo in each st—11 sts.

ALL SIZES
Rnd 4 (4, 4, 5): Work 1 ldc blo st to shift the beg of rnd. The following st will be counted as the first st of rnd. Ldc in each of the next 7 (8, 8, 9) sts, insert hook from top to bottom under horizontal strand of previous st, yo, and pull through lp (two lps on hook),

insert hook under back lp of next st, yo, and pull through to front of work (3 lps on hook), yo, and pull through all three lps, 1 sc blo in the next st—9 (10, 10, 11) sts.

SIZE WOMEN'S L/MEN'S S ONLY
Rnd 5: Sc blo in each st—10 sts.

ALL SIZES
Fasten off leaving a long tail. Using yarn needle, thread yarn tail through the flo of each of the remaining 9 (10, 10, 11) sts and pull tight to close hole in top of thumb.

Finishing

Use yarn tail at thumb to sew any gaps closed near where thumb meets hand. Use beg yarn tail at wrist edge to sew closed the small gap at beg of rnds. Weave in ends. Wet block if desired. Because this mitten was worked in a spiral, there is a small jog at the wrist edge. You can even out the wrist edge by blocking the mitten.

Aperture Scarf

DESIGNED BY KATHY MERRICK

This little neck wrap packs a lot of possibilities. Wear it as an ascot, as shown here; make it longer and it becomes a fabulous warm-weather scarf; seam it shut and you have a fabulous cowl. Plus, this project works up in a few hours so it's perfect as a last-minute go-to gift pattern.

FINISHED SIZE
35" long × 5" wide (89 × 12.5 cm) after blocking.
Motif: 5" (12.5 cm) in diameter.

YARN
DK weight (#3 Light)

Shown here: Zitron Patina (55% merino wool, 45% rayon; 120 yd [110m]/1¾ oz [50 g]): #5013 charcoal (MC); #5029 watermelon (CC), 1 ball each. Yarn distributed by Skacel Collection, Inc.

HOOK
Size G/6 (4 mm). Adjust hook size if necessary to obtain correct gauge.

NOTIONS
Yarn needle.

GAUGE
1 pattern rep = 2½" (6.5 cm). 7 pattern rows = 4" (10 cm) in Pattern Stitch, blocked.

NOTE
Motif is added to finished scarf.

2 SKEINS

2 Double crochet cluster (2dc-cl): [Yo, insert hook in indicated st or sp, yo, draw up a loop, yo, draw through 2 loops] twice, yo, draw through 3 loops on hook.

3 Double crochet cluster (3dc-cl): [Yo, insert hook in indicated st or sp, yo, draw up a loop, yo, draw through 2 loops] 3 times, yo, draw through 4 loops on hook.

4 Double crochet cluster (4dc-cl): [Yo, insert hook in indicated st or sp, yo, draw up a loop, yo, draw through 2 loops] 4 times, yo, draw through 5 loops on hook.

Pattern Stitch (multiple of 12 + 1)

Set-up row: (WS) Ch 13, sc in 2nd ch from hook; *ch 4, sk 3 ch, sc in next ch; rep from * to end.

Row 1: Ch 6, *sc in first ch-sp of previous row, ch 2, 7 dc in next ch-sp, ch 2, sc in next ch-sp, ch 5, rep from *, ending with ch 2, tr in last sc of previous row, turn.

Row 2: Ch 1, sc in tr, *ch 2, dc in next 3 dc, (dc, ch 3, dc) in next dc, dc in next 3 dc, ch 2, sc in next ch-5 sp; rep from * ending with sc in last ch-6 sp, turn.

Row 3: Ch 4 (counts as first tr), *ch 1, dc4tog (see Glossary) in next 4 dc of previous row, ch 5, 4dc-cl (see Stitch Guide) in ch-3 sp, ch 5, dc4tog in next 4 dc, rep from *, ending with ch 1, tr in last sc of previous row, turn.

Row 4: Ch 1, sc in tr of previous row, *[ch 5, sc in next ch-sp] twice, ch 5, sc in ch-1 sp; rep from *, ending with sc in top of beg ch-5 sp of previous row, turn.

Rep Rows 1–4 for pattern.

Motif

Ch 8, sl st to first ch to form ring.

Rnd 1: Ch 3, dc in ring, ch 2, [2dc-cl in ring (see Stitch Guide), ch 2] 10 times; 2dc-cl in ring, ch 1, hdc in first dc of rnd.

Rnd 2: Ch 1, (sc, ch 3) in each ch-3 sp around, ending with sc in last ch-3 sp, ch 1, hdc in first sc.

Rnd 3: Ch 1, (sc, ch 5) in each ch-3 sp, ending with sc in last ch-3 sp, ch 2, dc in first sc.

Rnd 4: Ch 1, 2 sc in first sp, (2 sc, ch 3, 2 sc) in each ch-5 sp, ending with (2 sc, ch 3) in same ch-5 sp as first 2 sc of round, sl st to first ch to join.

Rnd 5: Turn, sl st in ch-3 sp, ch 3, turn, 2dc-cl in same ch-3 sp, (3dc-cl [see Stitch Guide], ch 3, 3dc-cl) in each ch-sp around; end with (dc3tog, ch 3) in same sp as first cluster, sl st to top of first cluster.

Fasten off.

Scarf

With MC, ch 25. Work set-up row, then work Rows 1-4 twice, then Rows 1-3 once.

Next row make keyhole as follows: Ch 1, sc in first st, [ch 5, sc in next ch-sp] twice, ch 11, sk (dc4tog, ch-1, dc4tog), sc in next ch-sp, [ch 5, sc in next ch-sp] twice.

Next row: Ch 6, sc in first ch-sp of previous row, ch 2, 7 dc in next ch-sp, (ch 2, sc, ch 5, sc, ch 2) in ch-11 sp, 7 dc in next ch-sp, ch 2, sc in next ch-sp, ch 2, tr in last sc of previous row.

Work Rows 2-4 once.

Work 8 more pattern reps. Fasten off.

With CC, make motif.

MOTIF TRIM

With CC, ch 3, 4dc-cl in first ch, ch 11, [4dc-cl in 3rd ch from hook, ch 11) 4 times, sl st to back of motif at Rnd 1, ch 11, [4dc-cl in 3rd ch from hook, ch 11] 9 times; sl st to same spot on back of motif, ch 11, [4dc-cl in 3rd ch from hook, ch 11] 4 times, 4dc-cl in 3rd ch from hook. Fasten off.

Finishing

Wet block scarf and motif, if needed, to finished measurements.

With yarn needle and CC, sew motif to scarf, placing center of motif just below keyhole.

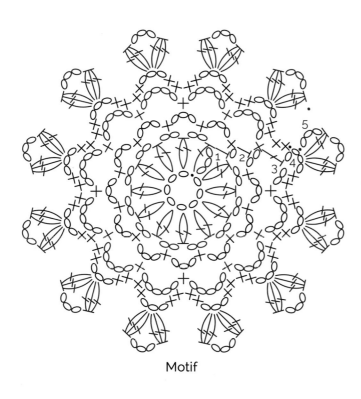

Motif

Pattern Stitch

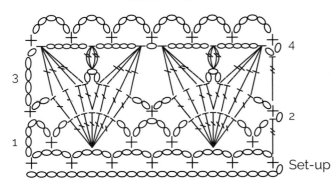

4

3

2

1

Set-up

- • = slip stitch (sl st)
- ○ = chain (ch)
- + = single crochet (sc)
- T = half double crochet (hdc)
- ǂ = double crochet (dc)
- ǂ = treble crochet (tr)

- ⋏ = double crochet 4 together (dc4tog)
- ⬭ = 2 double crochet cluster (2dc-cl)
- ⬭ = 3 double crochet cluster (3dc-cl)
- ⬭ = 4 double crochet cluster (4dc-cl)

Wavelength Beanie

DESIGNED BY SHARON ZIENTARA

This pattern is a great introduction to post stitches. It works up over just a couple of evenings, and if you're a more-experienced crocheter, the pattern is intuitive enough that it makes a good on-the-go project. This hat also happens to be my favorite type of accessory. It's perfect for a man because it isn't overly fussy, but a woman may just want to make one (or more) for herself, too.

FINISHED SIZES
18½ (20, 22¼)" (47 [51, 56.5] cm) in circumference.

Shown in size 20" (51 cm).

YARN
DK weight (#3 Light)

Shown here: Manos del Uruguay Silk Blend (30% silk, 70% extra fine merino wool; 150 yd [137 m]/1¾ oz [50g]): #3059 kohl (C), 2 skeins. Yarn distributed by Fairmount Fibers.

HOOK
Size F/5 (3.75mm). Adjust hook size if necessary to obtain correct gauge.

NOTIONS
Yarn needle.

GAUGE
19 sts and 28 rows = 4" [10 cm] in sc in the round after blocking.

2 SKEINS

Beanie

Ch 88 (96, 104) sts, sl st in beg ch to join for working in the rnd, being careful not to twist ch.

Rnd 1: Sc in 2nd ch from hook and in next 64 (70, 76) ch, pm in 65th (71st, 77th) st, [sc in next ch, dc in next ch] to end of rnd, sl st in first sc to join.

Rnd 2: Ch 1 (does not count as st throughout), 2 sc in first sc, sc to 2 sts before marked st, sc2tog, [sc in next sc, FPdc in dc from rnd below, sk sc behind FPdc] to end, sl st in first sc to join—88 (96, 104) sts.

Rnd 3: Ch 1, sc in each st around, sl st in first sc to join.

Rep Rnds 2 and 3 until hat measures 5" (12.5 cm).

Next rnd: Rep Rnd 3.

Dec rnd: Ch 1, [sc in next 19 (21, 23) sc, sc3tog over next 3 sts, pm in sc3tog] 3 times, [sc, FPdc in dc from row below] to last 3 sts, FPsc3tog (see Stitch Guide) in last 3 sts, sl st in first sc to join.

Next rnd: Ch 1, sc in each st around, sl st in first sc to join.

Next rnd: Ch 1 [sc to 2 sts before marked st, sc3tog over these 2 sts and marked st] 3 times, move marker to sc3tog, [sc in next sc, FPdc in FPdc from row below] to last 3 sts, FPsc3tog over last 3 sts, sl st in beg st to join.

Rep last 2 rnds until 40 sts remain.

Next rnd: Ch 1, sc in each st around, sl st in first sc to join.

Next rnd: Continue to rep decrease rnd every rnd until 8 sts remain. Fasten off leaving a tail to sew top of hat closed.

Bottom Ribbing

Join yarn with a sl st in any st on bottom of hat.

Row 1: Ch 6, turn.

Row 2: Sc blo in 2nd ch from hook and in next 4 ch, sl st in same st as join and in next 2 sts on edge of hat, turn.

Row 3: Ch 1, sc blo in each st across, turn.

Row 4: Ch 1, giving ch st a little tug to make a neat and tidy edge, sc blo in each sc blo, sl st in same st as join and in next 2 sts on edge of hat, turn.

Rep Rows 3 and 4 around entire bottom edge of hat. Fasten off leaving a tail to sew seam of ribbing tog.

Finishing

Weave in ends. Block.

Cirque Shawlette

DESIGNED BY CRISTINA MERSHON

This shawlette is a bold, funky statement piece. The jewel tones of the yarn create a dazzling effect. Just throw it over a plain T-shirt and jeans and let the crochet take center stage. For something less dramatic, try working the design in a solid color instead.

FINISHED SIZE
About 40" wide × 20" long (101.5 × 51 cm) without fringe. The final pattern is one size fits all, but it can easily be adjusted by adding or subtracting rounds.

YARN
Fingering weight (#1 Super Fine)

Shown here: Schoppel Wolle Zauberball (75% virgin wool, 25% nylon; 459 yd [420 m]/3½ oz [100 g]) #1536 fuchsienbeet, 2 balls. Yarn distributed by Skacel Collection, Inc.

HOOK
Size B/1 (2.25 mm). Adjust hook size if necessary to obtain correct gauge. Correct gauge is not crucial.

GAUGE
21 sts and 14 hdc blo rows = 4" (10 cm).

NOTES
The shawlette is constructed from top to bottom starting in the middle. The fringe of dangling motifs is worked all in one piece as the last row.

Unless otherwise indicated, dc stitches are worked in back loops only to create the ridge effect.

2 SKEINS

Large Fringe Circle: 30 tr in 6th ch from hook, sl st in first tr, at the same time trapping rem main foundation ch in sl st. Working along the foundation ch towards the body of the shawlette, work sc in every ch across to last ch, sl st in last ch.

Small Fringe Circle: 21 dc in 4th ch from hook, sl st in beg ch; trapping foundation ch in sl st, sc in each rem ch of tassle to last ch, sl st in last ch.

Shawl

Ch 6, sl st in beg ch to form ring.

Row 1: [Ch 2, 5 hdc in ring] twice, turn—10 hdc.

Row 2: Ch 2, 2 hdc in next hdc, hdc in each hdc to ch-2 sp, (2 hdc, ch 2, 2 hdc) in ch-2 sp, hdc in each hdc across to last hdc, 2 hdc in last hdc, turn—16 hdc.

Rows 3–54: Rep Row 2—328 hdc after Row 54.

Do not fasten off.

Edging

Row 1: Ch 25, work Large Fringe Circle (see Stitch Guide), *hdc blo in next 10 hdc, ch 15, work Small Fringe Circle (see Stitch Guide), hdc blo in next 10 hdc, ch 25, work Large Fringe Circle**; rep from * to just before center ch-sp, hdc blo in each st to center ch-sp, 2 hdc in center ch-sp, ch 15, work Small Fringe Circle, 2 hdc in same ch-sp, hdc blo in next 3 sts, ch 25, work Large Fringe Circle, rep between * and ** across, ending with hdc blo in last sts of row, ch 25, work Large Fringe Circle, sl st in corner of shawl. Fasten off.

Finishing

Weave in ends. Block, making sure that the motifs lie flat.

Transverse Mitts

DESIGNED BY BETH NIELSEN

These graphic mitts are a great introduction to tapestry crochet, a more advanced crochet technique. In tapestry crochet, multiple colors or yarn are switched back and forth to create colorful motifs with a woven look. Make these mitts with contrasting colors for a bold pattern or tonal or neutral hues for a more subtle effect. Either way, they're a modern piece that's fun to make and to wear.

FINISHED SIZE
7" in circumference × 8" long (18 × 20.5 cm).

YARN
Worsted weight (#4 Medium)

Shown here: Brown Sheep Lamb's Pride Worsted (85% wool, 15% mohair; 190 yd [174m]/4 oz [113 g]): M173 wild violet (MC), M03 grey heather (CC), 1 skein each.

HOOK
Size I/9 (5.5 mm). Adjust hook size if necessary to obtain gauge.

NOTIONS
Yarn needle.

GAUGE
8 sts and 8 rows = 2" (5 cm) square in main st pattern.

NOTES
For the spiral, you can choose to join to the beg of each rnd and start a new rnd, or you can place a stitch marker at the beg of the rnd and simply work in a spiral without joining. If you don't have a stitch marker handy, I recommend the first method.

One yarn is worked in sc, while another is carried along work. To switch colors, work last yo of st in the next color.

To carry yarn, lay yarn over top of sts being worked into, then sc as usual, encasing carried yarn inside sts.

1 SKEIN

Mitt (make 2)

With MC, ch 30, being careful not to twist, sl st in beg ch to form a lp.

Rnd 1: Ch 1, sc in same st as joining, sc in each ch around, sl st to first sc (see Notes). Do not turn—30 sc.

Rnd 2: With CC, sc blo in each sc around, sl st in first st to join.

Rnd 3: With MC, sc blo in each sc around, sl st in first st to join.

Rnd 4: [MC sc blo in next 5 sts (carrying CC–see Notes), CC sc blo in next 5 sts] around, sl st in first st to join.

Rnd 5: Working in both lps, CC sc in first st, [MC sc in next 5 sts, CC sc in next 5 sts] twice, MC sc in next 5 sts, CC sc in last 4 sts, sl st in first st to join.

Rnd 6: CC sc in first 2 sts, [MC sc in next 5 sts, CC sc in next 5 sts] twice, MC sc in next 5 sts, CC sc in last 3 sts, sl st in first st to join.

Rnd 7: CC sc in first 3 sts, [MC sc in next 5 sts, CC sc in next 5 sts] twice, MC sc in next 5 sts, CC sc in last 2 sts, sl st in first st to join.

Rnd 8: CC sc in first 4 sts, [MC sc in next 5 sts, CC sc in next 5 sts] twice, MC sc in next 5 sts, CC sc in last st, sl st in first st to join.

Rnd 9: With CC (not carrying MC), sc blo around, sl st in first st to join.

Rnd 10: With MC, sc blo around, sl st in first st to join.

Rnd 11: With CC, sc blo around, sl st in first st to join.

Rnd 12: CC sc blo in first 4 sts, [MC sc blo in next 5 sts, CC sc blo in next 5 sts] twice, MC sc blo in next 5 sts, CC sc blo in last st, sl st in first st to join.

Rnd 13: Rep Rnd 7.

Rnd 14: Rep Rnd 6.

Rnd 15: Rep Rnd 5.

Rnd 16: [MC sc blo in next 5 sts, CC sc in next 5 sts] around, sl st in first st to join.

Rnd 17: With MC, (not carrying CC), sc around, sl st to first st to join.

Rnd 18: With CC, sc around, sl st in first st to join.

Rnd 19: With MC, sc blo around, sl st in first st to join.

Rnds 20–27: Rep Rnds 4–11.

SHAPE THUMB OPENING

Beg working in rows.

Row 28: Rep Rnd 12. Fasten off and cut both yarns.

Row 29: With CC, join with sl st in first st and rep Rnd 13, joining MC at color change. Fasten off and cut yarns.

Row 30: With CC, join with sl st in first st and rep Rnd 14, joining MC at color change. Fasten off and cut yarns.

Row 31: With CC, join with sl st in first st and rep Rnd 15, joining MC at color change. Fasten off and cut yarns.

Row 32: With MC, join with sl st in first st and rep Rnd 16, joining CC at color change. Fasten off and cut yarns.

Now working in rnds.

Rnd 33: Rep Rnd 17, joining with sl st at end of rnd to close thumb opening.

Rnds 34 and 35: Rep Rnds 18 and 19. Fasten off.

THUMBHOLE EDGING

Join MC at any point around thumbhole, ch 1, work 14 sc evenly around thumbhole, sl st in first ch to join.

Rnd 2: With CC, sc blo around, sl st in join.

Rnd 3: With MC, sc blo around, sl st in join. Fasten off.

Weave in ends with yarn needle; block if desired.

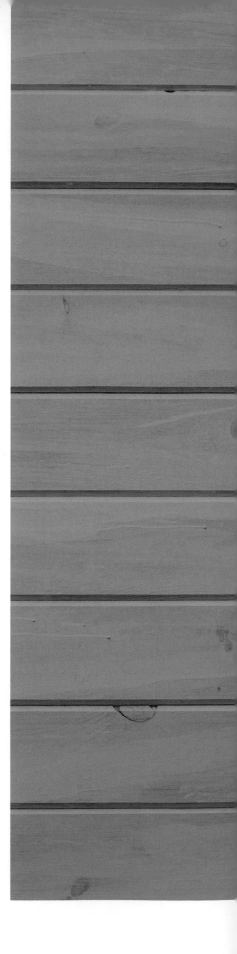

Enmeshed Cowl

DESIGNED BY JESSICA BOLOF

This luxurious cowl works up quickly in alternating columns of double, triple, and half double crochet separated by triple crochet sections. This project actually uses less than one skein of yarn, so you could easily lengthen the cowl to suit your taste.

FINISHED SIZE
27" in circumference × 7" deep (68.5 × 18 cm).

YARN
Worsted weight (#4 Medium)

Shown here: HiKoo Simplinatural (40% baby alpaca, 40% fine merino wool, 20% mulberry silk, 183 yd [167m]/3½ oz [100 g]): #098 bright blue, 1 skein. Yarn distributed by Skacel Collection, Inc.

HOOK
Size I/9 (5.5 mm).

GAUGE
12 tr and 4 tr rows = 4" (10 cm).

NOTES
This cowl uses a Foundation half double crochet (Fhdc) before working one section. Work is then turned upside down and worked upward.

Turning chs are not included in st counts.

Two skeins of Simplinatural will make three cowls.

1 SKEIN

Split treble cluster (str-cl):
Worked in 5 sts, yo twice, insert hook in first st, pull up loop, [yo, pull through 2 loops] twice, sk 3 sts, yo twice, insert hook in 5th st, pull up loop, [yo, pull through 2 loops] twice, yo, pull through 3 loops on hook. Next cluster is worked with first treble leg worked into same stitch as 2nd treble leg of previous cluster.

Cowl

Fhdc 80 (see Glossary), sl st in beg Fhdc to join in rnd being careful to avoid twisting sts.

Rnd 1: Ch 3, tr in each st around, sl st to beg st to join.

Rnd 2: Ch 2, hdc around, sl st to beg st to join. Fasten off.

SECOND SECTION

Turn work upside down and work following rnds from Fhdc bottom edge.

Rnd 1: Ch 3, [str-cl (see Stitch Guide), ch 3] around, sl st in beg st to join.

Rnd 2: Ch 2, hdc in each ch and str-cl around, sl st in beg st to join.

Rnd 3: Ch 3, tr in each st around, sl st in beg st to join.

Rnd 4: Ch 2, hdc around, sl st in beg st to join.

Rep Rnds 1–4 once more. Fasten off.

Finishing

Weave in ends. Block to measurements.

Abbreviations

beg	begin; begins; beginning	**pm**	place marker
bet	between	**rem**	remain(s); remaining
blo	back loop only	**rep**	repeat; repeating
CC	contrasting color	**rnd(s)**	round(s)
ch(s)	chain(s)	**RS**	right side
cl(s)	cluster(s)	**sc**	single crochet
cm	centimeter(s)	**sl**	slip
cont	continue(s); continuing	**sl st**	slip(ped) stitch
dc	double crochet	**sp(s)**	space(s)
dec	decrease(s); decreasing; decreased	**st(s)**	stitch(es)
dtr	double treble (triple)	**tch**	turning chain
est	established	**tog**	together
foll	follows; following	**tr**	treble crochet
g	gram(s)	**WS**	wrong side
hdc	half double crochet	**yd**	yard(s)
inc	increase(s); increasing; increased	**yo**	yarn over
lp(s)	loop(s)	*****	repeat starting point
MC	main color	**( )**	alternative measurements and/or instructions; work instructions within parentheses in place directed
m	marker; meter(s)		
mm	millimeter(s)	**[ ]**	work bracketed instructions a specified number of times
p	picot		
patt(s)	pattern(s)		

Glossary

Stitches

CHAIN (CH)

Make a slipknot and place it on crochet hook. *Yarn over hook and draw through loop on hook. Repeat from * for the desired number of stitches.

HALF DOUBLE CROCHET (HDC)

*Yarn over, insert hook in stitch (**figure 1**), yarn over and pull up loop (3 loops on hook), yarn over (**figure 2**) and draw through all loops on hook (**figure 3**); repeat from *.

figure 1

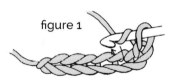

figure 2

figure 3

DOUBLE CROCHET (DC)

*Yarn over hook, insert hook in a stitch, yarn over hook and draw up a loop (3 loops on hook; figure 1), yarn over hook and draw it through 2 loops (**figure 2**), yarn over hook and draw it through remaining 2 loops on hook (**figure 3**). Repeat from *.

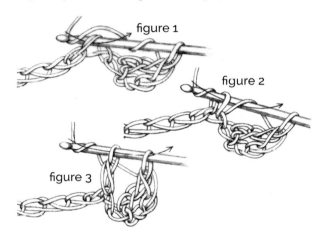

figure 1

figure 2

figure 3

TREBLE CROCHET (TR)

*Wrap yarn around hook twice, insert hook in next indicated stitch, yarn over hook and draw up a loop (4 loops on hook; **figure 1**), yarn over hook and draw it through 2 loops (**figure 2**), yarn over hook and draw it through next 2 loops, yarn over hook and draw it through the remaining 2 loops on hook (**figure 3**). Repeat from *.

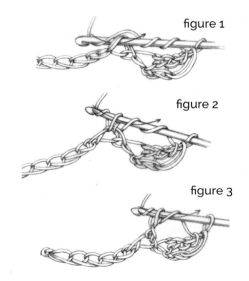

figure 1

figure 2

figure 3

EXTENDED SINGLE CROCHET (ESC)

Insert hook in next stitch, yarn over hook, draw up a loop (2 loops on hook), yarn over hook and draw through first loop on hook, yarn over hook and draw through both loops on hook—1 esc made.

DOUBLE TREBLE CROCHET (DTR)

Yarn over hook three times, insert hook in a stitch, yarn over hook and draw up a loop (5 loops on hook). [Yarn over hook and draw it through 2 loops] 4 times. Repeat from *.

FOUNDATION DOUBLE CROCHET (FDC)

Ch 3. Yarn over, insert hook in 3rd chain from hook, yarn over and pull up loop (3 loops on hook), yarn over and draw through 1 loop (1 chain made), [yarn over and draw through 2 loops] 2 times (**figure 1**)—foundation double crochet. Yarn over, insert hook under 2 loops of chain at bottom of stitch just made, yarn over and pull up loop (3 loops on hook) (**figure 2**), yarn over and draw through 1 loop (1 chain made), [yarn over and draw through 2 loops] 2 times (**figure 3**). *Yarn over, insert hook under 2 loops of chain at bottom of stitch just made (**figure 4**), yarn over and pull up loop (3 loops on hook), yarn over and draw through 1 loop (1 chain made), [yarn over and draw through 2 loops] 2 times. Repeat from * as needed (**figure 5**).

FOUNDATION HALF DOUBLE CROCHET (FHDC)

Ch 3, yarn over, insert hook in 3rd chain from hook, yarn over and pull up loop (3 loops on hook), yarn over and draw through 1 loop (1 chain made), yarn over and draw through all loops on hook—1 foundation half double crochet. *Yarn over, insert hook under the 2 loops of the "chain" stitch of last stitch and pull up loop, yarn over and draw through 1 loop, yarn over and draw through all loops on hook; repeat from * for length of foundation.

BACK POST SINGLE CROCHET (BPSC)

Insert hook from back to front, right to left, around the post of the specified stitch, yarn over hook, pull through work only, yarn over hook, and pull through both loops on hook—1 bpsc made.

BACK POST HALF DOUBLE CROCHET (BPHDC)

Yarn over hook, insert hook from back to front to back around post of corresponding stitch below, yarn over and pull up loop, yarn over hook and draw through all 3 loops on hook.

BACK POST DOUBLE CROCHET (BPDC)

Yarn over hook, insert hook from back to front, to back again around the post of stitch indicated, yarn over hook, draw yarn through stitch, [yarn over hook, draw yarn through 2 loops on hook] twice.

FRONT POST DOUBLE CROCHET (FPDC)

Yarn over hook, insert hook from front to back to front again around post of stitch indicated, yarn over hook and pull up a loop (3 loops on hook), [yarn over hook and draw through 2 loops on hook] twice—1 FPdc made.

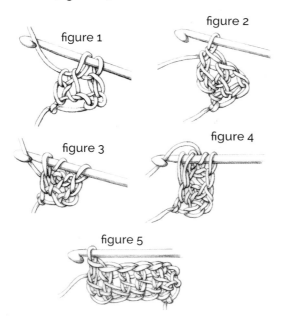

figure 1

figure 2

figure 3

figure 4

figure 5

FRONT POST TREBLE CROCHET (FPTR)

Yarn over hook twice, insert hook in specified stitch from front to back, right to left, around the post (or stem). Yarn over hook, pull through work only, *yarn over hook, pull through 2 loops on hook. Rep from * twice—1 FPtr made.

REVERSE SINGLE CROCHET (REV SC)

Working from left to right, insert crochet hook in an edge stitch and pull up loop, yarn over and draw this loop through the first one to join, *insert hook in next stitch to right (**figure 1**), pull up a loop, yarn over (**figure 2**), and draw through both loops on hook (**figure 3**); repeat from *.

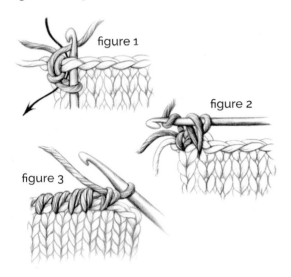

figure 1

figure 2

figure 3

Tunisian Crochet

TUNISIAN KNIT STITCH (TKS) IN THE ROUND

Insert hook under the vertical bar and to the back of the work, or between the front and back vertical bars, yarn over and pull up a lp.

In Tunisian in the round, there is no return pass (RetP); instead, with yarn on bobbin, and opposite end of hook as the one used to pick up loops, [yo, pull through 2 loops] as many times as necessary to work off the stitches you are picking up.

TUNISIAN PURL STITCH (TPS)

Forward pass (FwP): *Insert hook from right to left behind front vertical bar, yarn over and pull up loop, leave loop on hook; repeat from * to last vertical bar at edge, pick up front and back loops of last bar to create firm edge; return pass.

Return pass (RetP): Yarn over and draw loop through first loop on hook, *yarn over and draw though 2 loops on hook: repeat from * to end, ending with 1 loop on hook.

TUNISIAN SIMPLE STITCH (TSS)

Tss forward pass (FwP): *Insert hook from right to left behind front vertical bar (**figure 1**), yarn over and pull up loop (**figure 2**), leave loop on hook; repeat from * to last vertical bar at edge, pick up front and back loops of last bar to create firm edge; return pass.

Return pass (RetP): Yarn over and draw through first loop on hook, *yarn over and draw through 2 loops on hook (**figure 3**); repeat from * to end, ending with 1 loop on hook.

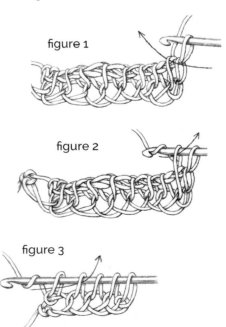

figure 1

figure 2

figure 3

Making an Adjustable Ring

Make a large loop with the yarn (**figure 1**). Holding the loop with your fingers, insert hook in loop and pull working yarn through loop (**figure 2**). Yarn over hook, pull through loop on hook. Continue to work indicated number of stitches in loop (figure 3; shown in single crochet). Pull on yarn tail to close loop (**figure 4**).

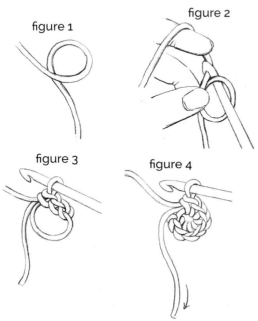

figure 1

figure 2

figure 3

figure 4

Decreases

SINGLE CROCHET TWO TOGETHER (SC2TOG)

Insert hook in stitch and draw up a loop. Insert hook in next stitch and draw up a loop. Yarn over hook (**figure 1**). Draw through all three loops on hook (**figures 2 and 3**)— one stitch decreased.

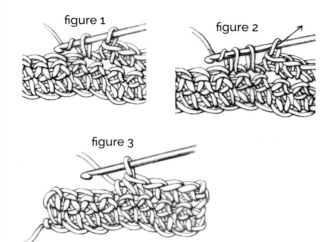

figure 1

figure 2

figure 3

SINGLE CROCHET THREE TOGETHER (SC3TOG)

[Insert hook in next stitch, yarn over, pull loop through stitch] 3 times (4 loops on hook). Yarn over and draw yarn through all 4 loops on hook. Completed sc3tog—2 stitches decreased.

HALF DOUBLE CROCHET TWO TOGETHER (HDC2TOG)

[Yarn over hook, insert hook in next stitch, yarn over hook and pull up loop] twice (**figure 1**), yarn over hook and draw through all loops on hook (**figures 2 and 3**)—one stitch decreased.

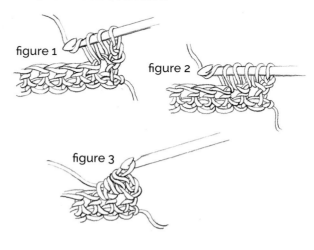

figure 1

figure 2

figure 3

DOUBLE CROCHET TWO TOGETHER (DC2TOG)

[Yarn over, insert hook in next stitch, yarn over and pull up loop (**figure 1**), yarn over, draw through 2 loops] 2 times (**figure 2**), yarn over, draw through all loops on hook (**figure 3**) —1 stitch decreased (**figure 4**).

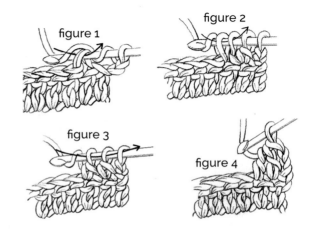

figure 1

figure 2

figure 3

figure 4

DOUBLE CROCHET THREE TOGETHER (DC3TOG)

[Yarn over, insert hook in next stitch, yarn over and pull up loop, yarn over, draw through 2 loops] 3 times (4 loops on hook), yarn over, draw through all loops on hook—2 stitches decreased.

DOUBLE CROCHET FOUR TOGETHER (DC4TOG)

[Yarn over hook, insert hook in next stitch, yarn over and pull up loop, yarn over and draw through 2 loops] 4 times, yarn over, draw through all loops on hook—3 stitches decreased.

EXTENDED SINGLE CROCHET TWO TOGETHER (ESC2TOG)

[Insert hook in next stitch, yarn over hook, draw up a loop (2 loops on hook), yarn over hook and draw through first loop on hook] twice, yarn over hook and draw through 3 loops on hook—1 esc2tog made.

Seaming

BLINDSTITCH

Slide threaded yarn needle in piece A for about ¼" (6 mm). *Poke the needle back out and directly in piece B. Repeat from * until needle is full of stitches, and then pull needle through until yarn is taut. Repeat around, snaking your needle back and forth between the two pieces. Your stitches should be hidden if done correctly.

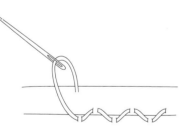

SINGLE CROCHET SEAM

Place the pieces together with the wrong (WS) or right sides (RS) facing, depending on whether you want your seam to be hidden on the wrong side or show on the right side of your work. Hold the pieces in your hand with the two edges facing you.

Insert the hook through both pieces at the beg of the seam and pull up loop, chain 1. Work a row of single crochet by inserting your hook through both pieces at the same time. Complete the seam and secure the end of the seaming yarn.

MATTRESS STITCH

With the RS facing, use threaded needle to *bring the needle through the center of the first stitch or post on one piece, and then through the center of the corresponding stitch or post of the other piece. Repeat from * to end of seam.

figure 1

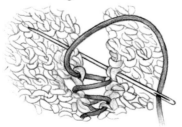

figure 2

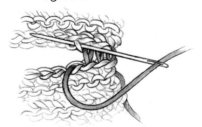

SLIP STITCH SEAM (SL ST SEAM)

To begin, place a slipknot on a crochet hook. With wrong sides (WS) facing together and working one stitch at a time, *insert crochet hook through both thicknesses in the edge stitches **(figure 1)**, grab a loop of yarn and draw this loop through both thicknesses, and then through the loop on the hook **(figure 2)**.

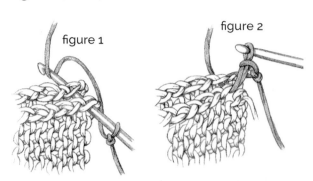

figure 1

figure 2

WHIPSTITCH

With right sides (RS) of work facing and working through edge stitches, bring threaded needle out from back to front, along edge of piece.

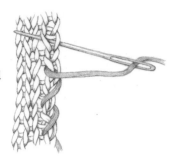

Embroidery

SLIP STITCH EMBROIDERY (SL ST EMBROIDERY AKA CH ST EMBROIDERY)

Bring threaded needle out from back to front at center of a stitch. Form a short loop and insert needle back where it came out. Keeping the loop under the needle, bring needle back out in center of next stitch to the right.

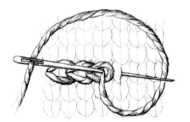

Sources for Yarns

BERROCO
1 Tupperware Dr., Ste. 4
North Smithfield, RI 02896
(401) 769-1212
berroco.com

BLUE SKY ALPACAS
PO Box 88
Cedar, MN 55011
(888) 460-8862
blueskyalpacas.com

BROWN SHEEP
100662 County Rd. 16
Mitchell, NE 69357
(800) 826-9136
brownsheep.com

CASCADE
cascadeyarns.com

CRYSTAL PALACE YARNS
160 23rd St.
Richmond, CA 94804
straw.com

DMC
77 S. Hackensack Ave., Bldg. 10F
South Kearny, NJ 07032-4688
(973) 589-0606
dmc-usa.com

MADELINETOSH
7515 Benbrook Pkwy.
Benbrook, TX 76126
(817) 249-3066
madelinetosh.com

MALABRIGO YARN
(786) 866-6187
malabrigoyarn.com

**MANOS DEL URUGUAY/
FAIRMOUNT FIBERS, LTD.**
P.O. Box 2082
Philadelphia, PA 19103
(888) 566-9970
fairmountfibers.com

ROWAN
Green Lane Mill
Holmfirth, West Yorkshire
England HD9 2DX
+44 (0)1484 681881
knitrowan.com
USA: Westminster Fibers
165 Ledge St.
Nashua, NH 03060
(800) 445-9276
westminsterfibers.com

**SKACEL COLLECTION, INC/
SCHOPPEL WOLLE/ZITRON**
PO Box 88110
Seattle, WA 98138
(800) 255-1278
skacelknitting.com

WISDOM YARNS/UNIVERSAL YARN
5991 Caldwell Park Dr.
Harrisburg, NC 28075
(877) 864-9276

About the Designers

BRENDA K. B. ANDERSON

Brenda K. B. Anderson makes mascots during the day. She cooks, crochets, and bellydances at night. She lives in a little house in Saint Paul with her awesome husband and their hairy baby, Mr. Kittypants. She is the author of *Beastly Crochet* and *Crochet Ever After.*

JESSICA BOLOF

Jessica is often found musing about her latest obsessions with sewing, yarn, and gluten free food at jessicabolof.com.

TERRI KELLER

Terri Keller was taught to crochet when she was young by her Granny Gaither and her daughter, Linda. As a military wife, mother of four grown children, grandmother of six, and owner of an English Mastiff named Thud, she has found her "happy place" in her love for all things fiber. She knits, crochets, spins, sews, and is getting ready to try her hand at bobbin lace.

KATHY MERRICK

Kathy Merrick taught herself to crochet from books and pictures. She sees new things and new details and fascinating ideas every day in her work. Crocheting feeds her endless curiosity about what happens if you add two more colors or if there is a way to connect motifs without big holes or how many ways can you put these chosen elements together. Along with what happens if you add ten more colors!

CRISTINA MERSHON

Cristina Mershon is a graphic designer by day and crocheter by night. She was born in Spain, in the small region of Galicia, where handcrafting has been a tradition for centuries. She loves creating classic crochet pieces with a modern twist, simple and flattering shapes, and elaborate edgings.

BETH NIELSEN

Beth Nielsen is a yarncraft-obsessed fashion designer, birth doula, and new mother in Chicago. In the summer she can be found at the farmer's market or rehabbing her craftsman bungalow. In the winter she swerves to avoid potholes and dreams about summer. Keep up with her at chicrochet.com.

ANASTASIA POPOVA

Anastasia Popova is a contributor to the soon-to-be-published *Fresh Design Crochet* book series by Cooperative Press. Her crochet career began when she designed and produced a line of kids' clothes and accessories for local boutiques. Catch up with Anastasia at anastasiapopova.com.

REGINA RIOUX

Regina leads a busy life juggling career, motherhood, and travel by day. By night, she is neck deep in yarn, imagining a crocheted world filled with possibilities. Her fingers are always busy designing and making things with string.

LINDA SKUJA

Linda Skuja is a founder of her crochet design brand Eleven Handmade. She's an award-winning designer specializing in stylish and modern designs. Linda enjoys developing crochet techniques in her own unique way. Visit her website to find out more: lindaskuja.com

Index

THESE INSPIRATIONAL RESOURCES FROM INTERWEAVE
will have you hooked!

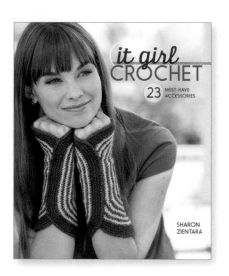

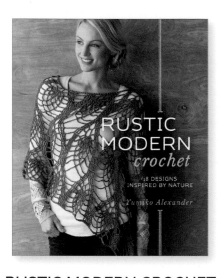